INSIDE MEN'S MINDS
YOUNG MEN TALK

Nick Fisher

Piccadilly Press · London

To Nellie

ACKNOWLEDGMENTS

Many thanks to Richard Ellingham for organising the
questionnaire. And thanks to all the readers of *Just
Seventeen* and *More!* magazines for their constant supply
of letters. And finally, a heartfelt thanks to all the men who
were brave enough to be interviewed and to answer my
questionnaire with such honesty.

The right of Nick Fisher to be identified as Author of this work
has been asserted by him in accordance with the Copyright,
Designs and Patents Act 1988.
Phototypeset by Spooner Graphics, London
Printed and bound by WBC, Bridgend, Mid Glam.
for the publishers Piccadilly Press Ltd.,
5 Castle Road, London NW1 8PR
A catalogue record of this book is available from the British
Library

ISBN 1 85340 188 9 (hardback)
ISBN 1 85340 193 5 (trade paperback)

Nick Fisher is British. he lives in Hackney, East London with his
wife called Helen, his whippet called Ollie and two rusty piles of
American engineering laughingly called 'cars'. He is a freelance
journalist, Agony Uncle, scriptwriter, and radio broadcaster. This
is his second book.

CONTENTS

INTRODUCTION

Very recently, I sat opposite a friend of mine in a restaurant while she talked about her errant boyfriend. He had been having an affair with another woman. He had confessed, then begged her to forgive him, (which, painfully, she did) then he went back to the other woman two weeks later. She was hurt and baffled.

"Why did he say he wanted to come back to me when he obviously didn't?" she asked. I had no answers. Then with a half-angry , half-despairing expression she announced "I just have no *idea* what goes on inside men's minds".

I write an advice column in *Just Seventeen*, have an agony slot on Radio 5 and write 'Mantalk' features for *More!* magazine. Every month I receive hundreds of letters from males aged between 13 and 30 and even more from females wanting to understand men.

I wanted to know more myself about what goes on inside men's minds, so I devised a questionnaire to send out to male readers across the country, which would give me a rough cross-section of how they would view themselves, women and the world.

Over forty men took the time and effort either to answer the questionnaire or sit through personal probing interviews to help provide a picture of what men think about certain subjects and situations.

And the result, in the form of this book, is by no means intended to be an exact science full of startling analysis and statistics. It's just a glimpse behind the normally shut curtains of some men's minds. Sometimes peeking inside is horribly predictable and depressing, other times it's refreshing and full of hope.

Nick Fisher

Chapter One

MEN GROWING UP

According to Freud the child is supposed to be the 'father of the man', so the influences to which the child is exposed at an early age are very important, and for most people, these come from their parents.

Our parents and the relationship we have with them can have a long-lasting effect on the way our characters and views of life develop. They can also have an effect on the way we relate to other people.

Most men's first male role-model is their father. Some fathers only perpetuate a lineage of male misconceptions and mixed messages about boys, whereas others take great pains to pass on something new and useful through the role of fatherhood.

WHEN YOU WERE A CHILD DID YOU HAVE A LOT OF RESPECT FOR YOUR FATHER?

Yes, because in my eyes my father had achieved everything: a good job, a house, a family and he was liked and respected in the community. He was also basically kind and compassionate.

Julian, 19

Yes, he was always very honest and fair.

Steve, 23

Yes. I thought he was brilliant. He was smart and tough and hard-drinking and funny.

Mark, 19

Yes, he was always there when I needed him.

David, 21

Yes, he achieved a lot in his working life but still had time for me.

Chris, 24

Yes, after my mum died when I was six it must have been very difficult but he managed to look after me and my sisters. I'm very proud of him now.

Kevin, 24

No, my father and I were not particularly close. Whenever I did something he always seemed to put me down, as if he resented me.

Philip, 20

No. He never just let me be me. He always had some code of conduct for me to live by.

Sean, 25

No. He treated me and my mum very badly. It's taken me a long time to realise and come to terms with this but I think he ruined my early life.

John, 24

Not much, he was extremely impatient and rude. He worked very hard but had very little time for us kids.

Gerry, 26

No. I wanted to differ in attitude and in behaviour — I didn't want to smoke as he did and I didn't want to be the typical man that he was.

Jonathan, 21

No, I think I'd have been better off without a father.

Lewis, 24

Answers to this question seem to be very black or white, with men seeming to either love or hate their dads. Either way, the feelings were obviously very strong and openly voiced.

Most of the men questioned were quite scathing about their current relationships with their fathers. They remembered them fondly in childhood but were dismayed by them as they themselves developed into adults. This is because men as adults have difficulty in relating to each other. The father becomes another male, not a father, and it is hard for most men to then have a relationship. In contrast, most men felt that their relationships with their mothers improved as they grew older.

WHICH OF YOUR PARENTS DO YOU HAVE THE BEST RELATIONSHIP WITH NOW AND WHY?

My mother, because I can talk to her about nearly anything that's happening in my life. My father's too difficult. Too judgmental.

Jonathan, 21

My mother overall. She takes an interest in what I'm doing. But my father doesn't even know — or care.

Martin, 22

Mum. Because she loves me and shows it.

Angus, 19

If I had to choose I'd say my mother. My dad gives me too much grief. He's the one who always says 'no'.

Lewis, 18

On a day-to-day relationship I'd have to say my mother. My father has always had my respect — yet my mother is the easiest one to live with.

Steve, 23

My mum is a pain. She's constantly on at me, especially during the holidays. She makes me get up and won't let me bring mates round the house when she's out. We fight a lot. I fight with my dad too, but usually Mum starts it.

Ryan, 18

Most of the men give the impression of their mothers being supportive and caring, but their fathers being either terribly distant or else very judgmental. They do often relate to their fathers through the sporting or leisure activities they share, but curiously, they feel more emotionally tied to their mothers.

Yet some do include their fathers in their nominations for childhood heroes.

WHEN YOU WERE A CHILD DID YOU HAVE ANY HEROES OR ANYONE YOU PARTICULARLY LOOKED UP TO?

My father was my hero while I looked up to Karl Heinz Rummenigge the West German international footballer due to his courage and skill.

Julian, 19

Kenny Dalglish (the footballer) and James Cagney.

Richard, 20

David Gower (cricketer).

Hamish, 21

Glenn Hoddle for his superb footballing skills and because he is a Christian.

Paul, 21

I look up to Eddie Vedder of Pearl Jam because he's an ass-kickin', baby kissin', sweet smellin' Rock God.

Nick, 18

My dad was my hero for many years because he seemed like the best bloke in the world. Then I really got into tennis and began to worship Bjorn Borg.

Aaron, 22

Bryan Robson.

Marcus, 23

Robert De Niro.

Kapil, 20

Arnold Schwarzenegger.

Victor, 19

James Joyce and Bobby Sands.

Liam, 29

*I never had heroes in a conventional celebrity sense.
The men I admired most were real, like a local
pheasant poacher I knew — oh and Barry Sheen,
I guess.*

Allan, 30

Fathers are initially the main influence in a male's life.
However, the peer group soon takes over. Particularly at
school, when boys start to hang around together in groups,
segregated (usually voluntarily) from girls, they start to
influence each other's behaviour and beliefs in a big way.

Relationships and friendships formed at school can be
long lasting and sometimes have a pronounced effect on a
man's development.

WHAT EFFECT DID YOUR SCHOOL DAYS HAVE ON YOUR LIFE AND CHARACTER?

*My secondary school days were superb. Primary
school was enjoyable and I think I was popular at
both. They gave me confidence.*

Mark, 19

*I realise now that they were the best days of my life —
everything was so easy! Adult life is a disappointment
in comparison.*

Sean, 20

I have good memories of my school days. I enjoyed the

*sport, the camaraderie and the sense of belonging.
They made me able to compete well in the world.*

Hamish, 21

*Overall it was OK — there was the odd bad teacher
but generally I enjoyed it. I was reasonably popular
unlike some poor bastards who were given a really
hard time. Looking back it scares me to remember
how cruel my peers could be.*

John, 24

*I look back and think it was brilliant. I wish it had
lasted longer. I seem to have had so many friends
then. There was something about school that spoiled
me for later life.*

Bryan, 28

*I was reasonably happy, probably because I had
a lot of friends, some of whom I still see these days.
Friendships were forged then and still remain strong.*

Michael, 25

*I didn't enjoy school at all. I was viewed as a nerd and
as a result I was not seen as one of the lads. It took me
a long time to shake this poor self-image off.*

Justin, 22

*I was picked on for being fat at school. I'm not fat any
more, but I will never forget the way I was treated. I
look back with hate.*

Ian, 24

*I was bullied non-stop for five years. Not surprisingly
this makes me very wary of my fellow man.*

Peter, 20

School was boring. Life is boring.

Chris, 18

*In a lot of ways school provided a very practical lesson
in life. There were a lot of boys who were faster, fitter,*

cleverer and better-looking than me. Now I'm an
adult, nothing's changed.

Martin, 22

Most men's memories of school seem to be tied up with
the quality of friendships they had, or treatment they
received from their male peers. No-one mentioned their
relationships with girls at school, although most of the
interviewees attended co-ed establishments.

Some boys seem to bond very well and very quickly at
school with each other. Often they're the sporty, activity-
orientated types who measure themselves in terms of their
achievements and popularity. Their success gives them a
sense of confidence and fearlessness which may stand
them in good stead in later life, but may also breed
insensitivity towards others' weaknesses and doubts.

On the other hand, being picked on and bullied through
your formative years can make you very scared of other
males, because you've already witnessed to your
discomfort how unfeeling they can be.

They do say that you can't choose your family but you
can choose your friends. So, the identity of the father role-
model that you start off with is out of your control, but
from then on it's up to you. But is this really true?

Early friendships were often about school and
geography. Where you lived and where you were educated
determined who you hung out with. And as a child, you
had no control over these situations.

For men as for women the earliest and most dominant
influence is their mother. However, men have the difficult
task that they must then cross over to their father's world.
At six or seven many find this a traumatic experience.
Although in the last fifteen to twenty years there has been
less emphasis on what is 'manly' and what isn't, one can
see from the men interviewed that most of them didn't
have a father or a role-model that really helped them.

Chapter Two

MALE FRIENDSHIPS

MALE FRIENDS

Women constantly marvel at the strangeness of male
friendships. A woman-friend recently told me about her
boyfriend's mate, whom he's known since college days
and whom he sees on a weekly basis. It transpired that the
mate's wife had left him a month previously, but he had
never said anything to his best friend. He only learned
about the situation when my friend – his girlfriend –
found out about it from another source.

It turned out that it was no great secret or even a source
of embarrassment to the friend that his wife had left him.
It was just never discussed. He either didn't want to or
didn't know how to talk about it. My female friend was
shocked. Her feeling was that if *her* best friend was having
even minor difficulties with her husband/boyfriend, then it
would be a constant topic of conversation. And if he had
walked out on her, as this man's wife had done, she would
expect to be told about it immediately and to provide
support in return.

Friendships between men don't necessarily function
along the same lines. Her subsequent question about this
situation was – 'If men don't talk about their intimate
relationships to each other, what *do* they talk about?'

WHAT DO YOU TALK ABOUT WITH YOUR FRIENDS?

*I don't really know. Everything, I guess. Except really
personal stuff.*

Martin, 22

Music, football, girls, computer games.

Ryan, 18

It depends on the friends. With some of them it's just chit-chat about college and football and other friends. With my close friends I talk about wider issues; philosophical things.

Darryl, 22

I tell my best friend everything; how I feel, when I'm happy, when I'm nervous or excited – everything.

Angus, 19

If there's a group of us out for a drink we usually talk about things we've done in the past – memorable nights out or events we all went to. Or maybe we plan the next event. No-one talks much about their private life. It would be difficult and no-one would be interested, or if they were it would be for the wrong reasons.

Paul, 21

Fishing and beer.

Lewis, 24

Any old bollocks.

Richard, 20

Most of my friends work out. So we tend to talk about weights, exercise and diets.

Vince, 19

Essex girls and WWF wrestling.

Maurice, 18

Books and films and music.

Justin, 22

I play five-a-side for a Works team. When we're not playing we talk about work – or maybe holidays or sometimes football, I guess.

Ian, 24

We talk about most subjects; news, politics, sport as well as personal things. Although there are definite no-go areas and things that no-one talks about. You sort of instinctively know what these are.

Raj, 21

Everything and nothing. Everything that's funny and nothing that's serious.

Gary, 22

Male friendships have a tendency to revolve around activities. A lot of men fuel and maintain their friendships by a common involvement like a sport, a hobby or work.

Men prefer to go out in groups, generally, whereas women prefer to go out with just one or two others.

When you're younger, friendships are often made through going to school together or living in the same area. As you grow older, those same friendships may continue, but in order to make new friends there often needs to be a common activity to focus the friendship. It's as though men need to be doing something together all the time because they find it so difficult to just sit and talk.

In many ways, the older you get the harder it is to make new friends. Men often seem to stick with their old friends and are quite guarded about meeting new men.   A lot of men don't really have friends, more acquaintances.

One reason for this may be that many men feel as though they are in continual competition even with their friends, so there is pressure on them to keep one step ahead.

School is the first place where peer pressure is brought to bear, and many boys find themselves competing against one another, trying to impress their mates, and generally attempting to be 'one of the lads'. And the sad thing is, this sort of behaviour doesn't always get left behind in the playground.

DO YOU FEEL A SENSE OF RIVALRY WITH YOUR MALE FRIENDS?

Yes, but it's not that extreme. At university it's expressed in physical or even computer games, but no-one gets that bothered.

Justin, 22

Yes, competition over games, like pool in the pub. But I think it hides a deeper sense of rivalry between us that doesn't come out in the open.

Julian, 19

I'm a very competitive person but I enjoy playing in a team with my mates – so the rivalry is really with other teams of people you don't know. But I suppose there is some rivalry to get in the 1st XV or score the most points or drink the most beer!

Peter, 20

No I don't think so – well certainly nobody shows it.

Patrick, 19

I don't want to but I do. And if the truth be known, the closer they are the stronger the rivalry feels. It's like a disease and spreads into every aspect of your life. I hate it, but I know it's there.

Allan, 30

Of course I feel rivalry. All men do. The ones who say they don't are either lying or copping-out. It's not that you necessarily want to compete. It's just that if you don't you've lost before you've started. The pressure is on from others.

Angus, 19

Friendship and rivalry are the same thing. It's not serious, but it is there – always.

Keith, 18

Part of the rivalry between friends is the business of trying to impress them. Men definitely want to be fancied by women and they usually want to be admired by society, but maybe most of all they want to have the approval and respect of their male friends. For some, this desire for respect will even go as far as wanting to be the object of envy amongst men.

IF YOU REALLY WANTED TO IMPRESS YOUR MATES, HOW WOULD YOU GO ABOUT IT?

I don't need to — they take me as I am.

Jeremy, 24

Make them laugh.

Gerry, 26

Turn up to the pub in a new car — although they'd probably think it was stolen.

Lewis, 18

Write a best-selling novel. Not a trashy Jeffrey Archer, but something cutting and relevant and funny. Something they'd read and think — this is brilliant!!

Liam, 29

Win loads of money at the bookies and then be extremely rude and crass.

Darryl, 22

Drink 12 pints in one session!

Adam, 19

Cop off with a beautiful woman.

Richard, 20

Get a date with Linda Lusardi.

Darryl, 22

Get seen out clubbing with Naomi Campbell or Beatrice Dalle.

Justin, 22

Win a trip round the world.

Ryan, 18

Do something heroic, like save some kid from drowning. If it was anything flash like winning the pools or marrying a film star I'm sure it would be closely followed by jealousy and I'd soon not have any mates left to impress.

Frank, 24

Women are the key to prestige amongst your friends. All men, quite wrongly, respect a promiscuous man. It's all part of the 'men are better than women' thing.

Gary, 22

They're such a sarky bunch it's probably impossible. A lot of my social life is based on slagging each other off — impressing each other is considered boring if not socially unacceptable.

Martin, 22

Get a trial for Arsenal.

Keith, 18

A sense of humour, a flash car and a desirable job score pretty highly amongst the suggested objects of envy, but the attentions of a beautiful and preferably famous woman score highest.

So, if you want to impress your friends, then one way of doing it is to have a beautiful girlfriend. But is this a statement about the value of a loving relationship, a testament to physical beauty or merely an example of women representing enviable possessions?

AMONG YOUR FRIENDS, HOW IMPORTANT IS IT TO HAVE A GIRLFRIEND?

Not now but maybe four or five years ago it was.

Philip, 20

Quite. If you have one it's something to be proud of but it's not essential for your social standing.

Richard, 20

It's almost unacceptable if you haven't got a relationship going. But I simply look for a girl when I want one. I won't be pressured into a relationship for the sake of it.

Darren, 19

We all tend to go round in couples — so I suppose it's pretty important.

Chris, 24

Depends on the girlfriend. Not if she's a dog.

Hamish, 21

It's not a big thing — or it shouldn't be. But I have heard some guys say things about other guys if they haven't been out with a girl like for a couple of years. I don't know how much of it is a joke and how much is true, but they either insinuate that they must be gay or 'latent' or at least terminally unattractive.

Liam, 29

I don't know, I've never really been without one, so I'm probably not the best to ask.

Allan, 30

Nobody really cares, but obviously a girlfriend shows you've got something.

Tim, 20

I think it's getting increasingly important. It's definitely important not to be a virgin.

Victor, 19

According to these men, it seems that a man can be a man even if he hasn't got a girlfriend, but not if he's got an ugly girlfriend or if the relationship is non-sexual.

So, if women are deemed to be objects of envy, does that mean that men will admit to having felt envious of other men's girlfriends?

HAVE YOU EVER BEEN JEALOUS OF A FRIEND BECAUSE OF HIS GIRLFRIEND?

Yes, because she was beautiful, but nothing happened.
Graham, 19

Yes, several times, but I never did anything about it. Jealousy is a part of life — we're continually being bombarded by images of beautiful things like cars, houses, material things as well as women but you just have to remember that it's all hype and to get on with your own life.
Andy, 25

Yes, a mate of mine copped off with a girl who was my friend. We had been just friends since I was 7, but I think I wanted it to be more than that. So when he started getting off with her, I hated them both.
Stephen, 18

Yeah, loads of my mates' girlfriends. They nearly all seem to be better than the girls I get.
Ryan, 18

No, because I've never seen one more gorgeous than mine. Honest.
Jonathan, 21

I've been envious of lots of them for having girlfriends, but not envious of the specific ones. I want one that is special for me.
Bryan, 19

The fact that women seem to represent an important role in most men's lives would suggest that they are a constant concern amongst men. Yet they don't feature very prominently in the subjects that men claim to talk about to each other.

A lot of women admit to spending a large amount of their time together talking about men and relationships. They find men hard to fathom and seek insight through discussion and comparison with their female peers. However, men aren't blessed with any automatic insight into the thoughts and behaviour of women, so why don't they discuss them in the same way?

DO YOU EVER DISCUSS WOMEN WITH YOUR MALE FRIENDS? DO THESE DISCUSSIONS INCLUDE RELATIONSHIPS OR SEX?

In a group of male friends the conversation is usually limited to general comments about women but I do discuss relationships and sex with my best friend.

Julian, 19

Yes, openly, frequently and on all accounts. I like to hear other men's stories too.

Kapil, 20

Yes, not obsessively but relationships or sex are not taboo.

Ian, 24

Yes, women and relationships but not sex. That should be between you and your lover and not discussed over a beer.

Philip, 20

Yes, but usually in a frivolous way. By that I mean discussing a girl's appearance or what your chances might be, rather than any problems in our own relationships. I couldn't see any of my mates describing any hydraulic or mechanical problems they had in bed down the pub.

Chris, 18

*There are some things you can say and some things
you can't. You have to know where to stop.*

Nick, 18

*Sure we talk about sex, but not really personal stuff,
just general about what it's like.*

Vince, 19

*We talked about girls and sex all the time when I was
a teenager, when none of us were actually doing it.
Now I'm older, we talk about cars and work mainly.*

Michael, 25

The impression I get from women is that they expect
men to talk graphically and lewdly about sex to each
other. They think that's one of those things that men do.
But in fact, in my experience they don't. Like the last
quote suggested, during adolescence there's much talk
about girls' bodies and sex technique, but most of it's
made up or cribbed from books.

By the time most men are having active sexual
relationships with women, they don't discuss it so much —
perhaps because it is now closer to them.

Men grow apart from their mates when they have a
serious relationship. It is harder for them to report the
deeper, more complex emotions an involvement with
another person entails. The dynamics of their relationship
with their mates change.

Envy in itself is a strange thing. Some men are happy to
admit to feeling it, while others talk as though it's a sin.

ARE YOU IN ANY WAY ENVIOUS OF OTHER MEN?

*Men that women see as attractive — men with 'perfect'
physiques.*

Julian, 19

Anybody more handsome, taller, fitter, richer or happier than me. The majority of men!

John, 24

Good singers and lyric writers earn my respect and admiration. Also men with thick long hair and spots.

Nick, 18

I'm very happy with the way I am but I suppose a better physique, good looks and a greater intellect would all be good.

Michael, 25

A real man is someone who knows himself. Someone who doesn't have to pretend or pose for the sake of other people. But then I suppose that's the same for a woman too.

Marcus, 23

I'm envious of confident men because they know what they want and have the confidence to do it.

Vince, 19

I am envious of successful businessmen — like Richard Branson — although it's more like respect. Particularly for the fact that he's young. I've set myself high targets and I know that I shall soon be successful in my own right.

Paul, 21

No, envy is a waste of time. It's an empty emotion.

Jeff, 28

If I felt envy towards a man I'd kill myself. We are what we are and if we want to be better then we all have an equal opportunity to go forward in life. Envy will rot you inside.

James, 21

I envy talent and skill. I'd love to have a talent or a

skill, be able to play the piano, or paint or drive a racing car. So I don't envy the person, just the talent.

Allan, 30

I envy Richard Gere for being married to Cindy Crawford.

Liam, 29

Rod Stewart, because of his voice, cars and girlfriends.

David, 21

Paul Gascoigne.

Darren, 19

There is definitely a pressure on most men not to reveal too much of themselves through fear of being abused and attacked by other men, often their friends.

It can be a major handicap if you want to ask questions or express emotions, but are too frightened to.

Sadly, one of the ways that men can express their anger and frustrations is through violence. Often those who have never actually been involved in a fist-fight will admit to fantasising about them. It's almost as though the inability to talk about things and deal with emotions in a verbal and comforting way necessitates 'letting off steam' in what are often totally inappropriate ways.

HAVE YOU EVER BEEN IN A FIGHT? HOW DID YOU FEEL ABOUT IT? WOULD YOU RESORT TO PHYSICAL VIOLENCE IF YOU NEEDED TO?

No, I've always avoided confrontation.

Jeremy, 24

No . . . well, I was beaten up a couple of times at school but you could hardly call it a fight. It depressed me that I couldn't do anything about it.

Nick, 18

Yes, twice . . . and both at school. Won one — lost one. Both were pretty horrible experiences, lots of adrenalin, lots of pressure from other boys to fight and both were about nothing very important. But I suppose I preferred the one I won — it gave me a bit of 'cred' among my mates.

Sean, 20

Yes, I was always fighting at school. I suppose I used to enjoy it in a way. I was certainly quite good at it and no-one got seriously hurt. But when I was seventeen I got involved in a fight in a pub where there were a lot of us drinking and it ended up with this guy pulling a knife and one of my mates got stabbed. He didn't die or anything but it shook me up. I'd never carry a knife but you don't know who might, so it's just too dangerous. Anyway I'm getting too old.

Peter, 20

Yes. Pathetic really. A fight at school. The whole thing was a farce — it didn't solve anything. The black eye I received got me a lot of stick even though I 'won' — if you can call it that.

Antonio, 23

Once and only once. I started it and I also managed to finish it by head-butting my opponent with my nose. A painful lesson.

Graham, 19

I've been involved in a few fights in pubs, which mainly involved a lot of pushing and shouting. Silly stuff, but frightening all the same.

Darryl, 22

DO YOU EVER FANTASISE ABOUT FIGHTING OR VIOLENCE?

*The worst situation is where you've had a shouting
match with someone and then later you play over in
your mind what you should have done to him. I do
that sometimes. It's embarrassing but I re-enact what I
should have done; where I should have hit him and
what I should have said. It's mad.*

Justin, 22

*The other day I got into an argument with a taxi
driver. He threatened to stick an umbrella up my arse.
I still can't help thinking about beating him up. I wish
I knew karate or something.*

Ian, 24

*I fantasise about catching the guys who stole my
mountain bike and what I'd do to them.*

Maurice, 18

*I never just fantasise about war or murder, but I do
dream about being able to win fights against men
who get in my way.*

Martin, 22

*I have this fantasy about an armed robber smashing
into the office where I work and holding up the staff,
maybe even taking one of the juniors hostage, and I
disarm him in front of everyone. Sort of being a hero.*

Gerry, 26

*I sometimes pretend I've got a gun in my pocket and
I can shoot bad people.*

Gary, 22

*Dreaming about punching someone's lights out is a
common occurrence with me. Even if it's one of my
friends. It's all right because I know it's just a dream,*

it'll never become a reality and it seems to make the aggravation better.

Jason, 25

Dreaming about punching your best mate's lights out does seem like a strange way to conduct a friendship. But in a lot of ways it's just evidence of how the inter-male communication system works. Rather than being able to talk about and process difficult feelings around a situation with a friend, a violent fantasy gets acted out internally in an attempt to exorcise the feelings. And indeed, it is far easier to have a no-holds-barred battle in your head than actually have to voice your true doubts and feelings.

For a lot of men, it simply isn't easy to talk to other men about personal things.

Men seem to have a much richer fantasy life than women. Look at any small boy and see him fighting and making battle noises. Men don't lose this and it could be the way many work through their problems. Women will always talk to a friend. Men can 'battle' things through in their mind.

IF YOU HAD A PERSONAL PROBLEM WOULD YOU BE MORE LIKELY TO TALK TO A MALE FRIEND OR A FEMALE FRIEND?

A female friend. I can't see a man taking the time to listen.

Tim, 20

Female of course. They are more compassionate. A male friend's quite likely just to laugh.

Vince, 19

A female friend or, depending on the subject matter, my mother.

Chris, 24

Female, they're more understanding.

Nick, 18

I could talk to a male friend, but how would I know he'd be sympathetic? A female friend would be.

Justin, 22

I'd talk to my girlfriend.

Keith, 18

The way male friendships seem to work is that other men are important to hang around with, to compete with and to emulate to some degree, but female friends are the ones that (if desperate) you turn to in times of personal and emotional troubles.

There is something fundamentally unsatisfactory about male friendships. It is as though they can function perfectly well on a superficial level but as soon as you want to go any deeper or broaden the range of topics, emotions and confidences you wish to share, you can quickly meet up with resistance and fear.

Men, it seems, are basically very frightened of getting close to each other; whether this is some sort of homosexual fear or simply a fear of unknown and uncharted areas, is not clear. But whatever the reasons, it means there is a marked lack of unity and understanding amongst men which, apart from anything else, makes changing the situation very difficult.

Chapter Three

WHAT MEN THINK OF THEMSELVES

I recently asked a few women to sum up their views about men very concisely: 'arrogant', 'arseholes', 'screwed up' and 'weird' were the most common negative appraisals. 'Exciting', 'strange', 'enigmatic' and 'annoying but good annoying' were the slightly more positive replies.

Most women did agree that men were basically a mystery. What goes on inside their minds and why they choose to do the things they do and behave the way they behave is largely incomprehensible. But they all seemed to think that men knew exactly who they were and what they were doing, they just chose not to communicate it to women. But do they?

Personally I'm of the belief that men are as big a mystery to other men as they are to women.

WHAT DO YOU THINK IT MEANS TO BE MALE?

To provide, lead and love is still the bottom line for most males.

Robert, 19

To be the dominant partner, in other words pay for things, as well as shaving and doing sports!

Martin, 22

To be the dominant one.

Raj, 21

A hard life.

David, 21

To be as hard as nails, as fit as a lion and quick in the head.

Nick, 18

To provide and protect.

Richard, 20

To be strong and smart and territorial.

Sean, 25

The traditional opinions are changing and I don't think there's anything very special about masculinity any more.

Kevin, 24

Not a lot these days.

Adam, 17

Bollocks.

Lewis, 18

So much has been written about this subject recently, you know, the New Man and all that, that I think it's difficult to know what it means — except that it's a lot more difficult than it was a few years ago when men had a more clearly defined role laid down for them.

John, 24

The role of masculinity is changing due to social and economic circumstances. As a woman's status has shifted and changed, so there have been new demands made on men. There is undoubtedly a lot of confusion among men as to what or who they are supposed to be, but the view that masculinity has got something to do with power is still very widespread.

Men do have some sense of what power is and what it means in terms of a man's status and attraction to the opposite sex.

WHAT IN YOUR OPINION MAKES A MAN POWERFUL?

Respect from others combined with authority.

Julian, 19

Knowledge, intellect, astuteness and having no qualms about hurting people along the way.

Paul, 21

What makes a man more powerful than another is his belief in himself, his self-esteem. This will dictate how he copes with the trials of life.

Angus, 19

Money, it's as simple as that.

Ian, 24

The bottom line is physical strength. The fact that most men can beat up most women is the basis of the difference between the sexes.

Stephen, 18

A good woman.

Marcus, 23

His mind and the way he uses it.

Sean, 25

Power is about money and possessions and status and all that, but it's also a sort of aura. Powerful men can make a room go quiet. They can command attention. People are a bit scared of them.

Keith, 18

To me power is muscle. Muscle is gained by sweat and hard work. Muscle comes from paying your dues.

Jonathan, 21

If power is perceived as a positive quality to most men, then presumably weakness must be seen as a negative one.

WHAT MAKES A MAN WEAK?

Living with a woman.

Frank, 24

A lack of belief in oneself and a lack of ability to control, survive or handle different situations.

Julian, 19

Having any qualms about hurting people.

Paul, 21

Not sticking up for yourself. Using and abusing others.
Gerry, 26

Not standing up for something you believe in.
Michael, 25

I think that when a man doesn't know what he wants and tries desperately to please everyone around him like his mother, father, girlfriend and friends then he becomes seriously weak.

Chris, 18

Lack of discipline and self-will.

Victor, 19

Sucking up to people.

Nick, 18

Drink, drugs and sex.

Robert, 19

Women. Mothers especially.

Darryl, 22

There are some strange contradictions among the men's views of masculinity and power, most notably that a good woman can make you strong, but women can also make you weak, and that caring about other people's feelings can be a sign of power as well as a sign of weakness.

There is, without a doubt, an ethos about masculinity (promoted by women as well as men) that favours the 'strong silent type'. In other words, to be physically powerful but emotionally in control is good, to be a weak, whining blabber-mouth is bad.

Fair enough, but what's a man supposed to do when he needs a good moan?

DO YOU THINK IT'S ALL RIGHT FOR MEN TO SHOW THEIR FEELINGS? WHAT WAYS OF SHOWING FEELINGS ARE ACCEPTABLE? IS IT ALL RIGHT FOR MEN TO CRY?

Yes, we're only human.

Richard, 20

After Gazza's tears in the World Cup everybody's doing it.

Justin, 22

Showing feelings outwardly is completely acceptable. Only extreme emotions, for example rage, should be kept in check for fear of insulting or hurting others.

Jeff, 28

It's now perfectly acceptable but I think it's got to be done with style.

Aaron, 22

Certainly. Tears of joy or despair are OK but anger is not really possible because it usually involves violence.

Jason, 25

It's all the rage these days for public figures to make emotional public displays which can get a bit sick-making, but I suppose it's better than the traditional British 'stiff upper lip'.

Sean, 25

Yes, why not? It's neither feeble nor feminine.

Jeremy, 24

If men say, 'I never cry', they are both liars and hypocrites.

Mark, 19

If you are going to cry, that is something you should do in the privacy of your own room. No-one wants to be seen to cry by their friends and it'll make their friends disrespect them.

Vince, 19

The whole idea behind the notion that 'big boys don't cry' suggests that it's unmanly and weak to shed a tear. Paul Gascoigne, in the World Cup, broke new ground by crying openly on TV in front of millions. But of course it was a matter of national pride and football, it wasn't because his girlfriend had chucked him or his pet dog had died.

Nobody really seems to be that against men crying as a concept, but the practice of it is a different matter.

HAVE YOU EVER CRIED IN FRONT OF YOUR FRIENDS? WHAT WAS THEIR REACTION?

No, but I wouldn't rule it out.

Robert, 19

No, and I don't think I would if I could help it.

Aaron, 22

No, far too embarrassing.

Justin, 22

No I haven't, but I wouldn't be ashamed to.

Tim, 20

Yes, once when I was pretty pissed and my girlfriend had just left me. My mates were really good about it, although they were pissed too, but we just ended up deciding that she wasn't worth it and slagging women off in general.

Antonio, 23

Yes, and they were totally sympathetic.

Julian, 19

Yes, but only when I broke my leg at rugby. I was crying and screaming with pain. That was all right. It made them realise how much it hurt.

Steve, 23

Yes, but only in front of friends who I knew wouldn't ridicule or laugh at me. Most guys are too stupid to understand.

Philip, 20

Yes, they went completely quiet, offered no support and seemed very awkward. It was as if they had never encountered anyone crying before.

Jeff, 28

Not that I can remember — and that saddens me. I can certainly remember a lot of occasions when I've cried on my own or with a woman, but none when I've cried with a male friend. I think that says something about the superficiality of male friendships.

Allan, 30

As a sort of macho rule of thumb, it's all right to cry in front of your mates if you've got something extraordinarily painful to cry about. Preferably it should be something physical as opposed to emotional.

Another concern men have is how the world perceives them.

WHAT SORT OF 'FIRST IMPRESSION' DO YOU MAKE AND DO YOU THINK IT'S A FAIR REPRESENTATION OF YOUR PERSONALITY?

Friendly, charming and witty. Yes, I think that's fair.
Angus, 19

I make sure I make a good first impression.
Jonathan, 21

I do all the stuff: firm handshake, open inviting smile, good eye contact. I reckon I cut quite a dash.
Martin, 22

I definitely interest people. They can't make me out. My style is quite original and my manner is quite cool. Sometimes I think people are a bit scared of me or in awe of me. I like that. I like to keep them guessing.
Raj, 21

Women respond well to me. I've got a good jaw line. I can soon tell from her eyes if she's impressed.
Peter, 20

I'm not sure — probably an arsehole!
Philip, 20

I think first impressions are very unfair. I know that I look like a complete idiot and people always assume that I am one but it just isn't true. It always takes a while before people see me for what I really am.
Aaron, 22

It all depends on who I'm meeting. I can come across as quiet and shy or noisy and stupid. But the problem

*is that people form vastly different opinions of me —
sort of Jekyll and Hyde.*

Pat, 19

*Lousy, lousy. I'm not very confident at all. First
impression I always feel I'm saying the wrong things
or coming across as a real jerk.*

Chris, 18

Most of the men seem to think that there is some sort of
perfect formula of looks and manner that makes them
come across as attractive and acceptable.

This idea of there being a perfect formula, is echoed in
some men's view of women and dating. I've received a
vast number of letters over the years from young men
wanting to know if there are any fail-safe chat-up lines that
will work. So, without the perfect formula chat-up lines,
what makes men feel embarrassed?

WHAT MAKES YOU FEEL EMBARRASSED AND HOW DO YOU COPE WITH IT?

*Arguments between my parents are really
embarrassing. I just wish I wasn't in the room. I don't
cope very well at all and usually end up leaving the
room.*

Nick, 18

*Saying stupid things. I usually go red and then try and
laugh it off.*

Angus, 19

*Saying the wrong thing. As soon as I realise it, I just
start apologising profusely.*

Jonathan, 21

When girls talk dirty about boys and sex.

Chris, 18

Meeting a girlfriend's parents. I don't know why but I automatically feel guilty, so I leave it as long as I can. I have to be very serious about her before I'll meet the family.

Antonio, 23

A stunning girl, the first time I meet her I get embarrassed. Sex talk doesn't embarrass me any more.

Gary, 22

Not having any money. I'm so pissed off with being poor. Most of my friends have got jobs and I'm a student. I feel like a charity case. It ruins my self-confidence.

Stephen, 18

Interviews, speeches and speaking to strangers. I cope by trying to get people to laugh or laugh with me.

Vince, 19

I sometimes have this nightmare where I fart really loudly at a graduation ceremony. I know it sounds funny, but in the dream I'm really ashamed.

James, 25

I went to a wedding do and everyone was in suits except me. I stuck out like a sore thumb. I felt everyone was laughing at me. I just wanted to leave.

Darryl, 19

When my girlfriend gets pissed. She can really make a scene or else go round telling everyone that she really, really loves them.

Ian, 24

Getting wet drips down the front of light trousers when you've just had a piss — then having to walk back into a crowded pub or restaurant.

Gary, 22

People complimenting me while I'm present. I just smile and act flattered, which I usually am!

Kapil, 20

Making social gaffes, saying stupid things and not having enough money are common sources of embarrassment for men. And one of the things they often do to get over the business of saying the wrong thing is to say nothing. It all fits in with the 'strong and silent' ethos – that it's better to say nothing and be mysterious than prattle on and make a fool of yourself.

And the thing about staying silent is that you never know, women might be fooled into believing that you're not just quiet, you might actually be a very 'deep' personality. And being 'deep' is something that a lot of men have come to believe that women find attractive in a man.

But what women really find attractive according to the surveys is a sense of humour.

HOW WOULD YOU DESCRIBE 'A SENSE OF HUMOUR' AND HOW IMPORTANT DO YOU THINK IT IS?

A sense of humour is the ability to laugh at what is around you, but most importantly at yourself. It's essential; life's too short to be taken seriously.

John, 24

Being able to see the funny side of things. It's absolutely vital.

Steve, 23

Laughing at life, your troubles and yourself. Essential, otherwise you'd go mad.

Gary, 22

It's an essential part of a personality. It can make or break a person — the ability to turn any situation, however disastrous, into a laughing matter. As long as it's not done sarcastically, it can create.

Hamish, 21

It's important to be able to laugh at yourself. Men don't find that easy.

Mel, 23

A sense of humour's about what you find funny. Some people don't find anything funny. In my opinion they tend to be very lonely people. Having a good laugh's about having a love of life. If you can't laugh you might as well be dead.

Keith, 18

It's very important because, let's face it, the world is a joke!

Chris, 18

One of the attributes that many respondents mentioned as being important in making a man attractive to women was assertiveness and self-assurance. Men often assume that they are expected to be assertive in certain situations.

DO YOU ASSERT YOURSELF IN SITUATIONS WHERE YOU THINK SOMEONE IS TAKING ADVANTAGE OF YOU?

I think I have a good understanding of my rights as a consumer. If I wasn't being treated fairly then I would definitely state my case. No-one will defend you unless you defend yourself.

Amion, 23

If someone's trying to have one over on me then I'll stand my ground even if it means a fight.

Jonathan, 21

I try to be, but in truth I get really nervous. I hate causing a scene and I hate it when everyone looks round to see who's causing a fuss.

Philip, 20

Yes, but it would have to be a pretty serious situation. But once I'm off, God help them.

Sean, 25

If I'm out with my girlfriend I don't have to bother, she complains for England so I just let her do it.

Paul, 21

Yes, where the person is unjustified in taking advantage of me. With friends I don't mind as I like doing favours for them.

Julian, 19

No. My middle name's 'door-mat'.

Sam, 24

The truth is that many men are not assertive or powerful and are basically very shy and scared about a lot of things in life.

Some men cope with their shyness or doubt by over-compensating and becoming loud and aggressive as a way of dealing with their fears. Others shrink away from anything that might cause a scene.

Some even escape the reality of such scary situations by indulging in fantasies of fame and fortune.

WOULD YOU LIKE TO BE FAMOUS?

Yes, I have two ideals: to be a world-famous footballer or be famous for doing something positive for the world.

Vince, 19

Most definitely. I want to prove myself in commerce

and being famous is the ultimate recognition for a businessman.

Jonathan, 21

I think it's all I want.

Graeme, 18

I would like to be a famous nurse. I don't want to end my life thinking that I was nothing. I want to achieve the absolute peak of my career.

Julian, 19

Rich and famous has always sounded good but just rich would do.

Stephen, 18

Sometimes I wish I was, but famous people get a lot of stick. Sometimes I'm glad I'm not. A few years ago I'd like to have been a pop star or a footballer but now I suppose it's a writer or someone creative like Andrew Lloyd Webber — that would be interesting.

Jason, 25

Not really, I would like the respect of my peers and to be very successful at whatever I do but I wouldn't want to be a 'household name' continually in the public eye.

Kevin, 24

No, it's a hugely overrated state.

Aaron, 22

No. I'm happy with who I am.

Richard, 20

Most men admit to having fantasies about being famous. However, in reality, although they wanted to achieve, success was not seen in terms of being famous.

After the dizzying heights of success and fame there is the darker side of life — fear. Fear is one of those 'unmanly' feelings that it's not too cool to show. But all men feel fear to some degree relating to different things. Fear can be a great motivator as well as a limiter in terms of behaviour. Sometimes a good amount of fear can be a healthy feature as it stops men from doing too many stupid things, whereas a severe fear of emotional rejection can have a socially crippling effect.

WHAT WOULD YOU CONSIDER TO BE YOUR GREATEST FEAR IN LIFE?

Being lonely, although sometimes I prefer my own company.

Philip, 20

To be lonely and alone. To be desperate for other people, particular women's company and to be denied it. Or being locked in prison. It's the same thing.

Liam, 29

To be raped by a man - or a gang of men.

Allan, 30

Being a failure at everything, not living up to my own expectations of my ability.

Mark, 19

Cancer.

Andy, 25

Dying of AIDS.

Victor, 19

Going to prison for a crime you didn't commit.

Nick, 18

Dying.

Ryan, 19

Death, because it might be so sudden. It seems strange that we're on this world for however many years and then we die and it's goodbye world. It's depressing.

Sean, 25

Dying before Manchester United win the league title again.

James, 21

Dying young.

Frank, 24

Getting victimised and beaten up by police.

Kapil, 20

Losing my dick.

Vince, 19

As a rugby player I would hate to end up paralysed and have to spend the rest of my life in a wheelchair – but it doesn't stop me playing rugby!

Richard, 20

Being stuck in an unruly mob or a crowd disaster like Hysel Stadium.

Jason, 25

Both my parents dying without having the chance to talk to them first.

Marcus, 23

Going mad.

Mike, 25

Catching HIV.

Morgan, 19

Losing my eyesight.

Pat, 17

Losing my dog.

Jeremy, 24

Growing up and being just like my dad.

Hamish, 21

Growing old on my own, with no-one to care for me and no money.

Kevin, 24

That I'll never be a success.

Antonio, 23

Letting other people down.

Darryl, 22

Whatever it is that a man fears most, is a reflection of what he values in his life. It's also perhaps some sort of key to what he thinks it means to be male.

Not surprisingly, most men said that their greatest fear involved loss or death or failure, with death being the most feared.

Surprisingly, I receive more letters from men who have worries and fears about their bodies than I do from women, and the number of letters is on the increase. The most frequent letter is from teenage boys embarrassed about what they perceive to be the inadequate size of their penis. The next two most common concerns are being too short and being too fat.

As weight-training and body-building become more popular and accepted leisure activities, and as the male fashion industry becomes more powerful, men seem to be becoming increasingly concerned with their looks and physique.

WOULD YOU SAY YOU WERE GENERALLY HAPPY OR UNHAPPY ABOUT YOUR BODY?

Very happy, content with what I've inherited and I make sure I look after it.

Michael, 25

I'm happy about the muscle definition and tone, but I'd be more keen to have extra height. It would equal out my proportions. If I continue to maintain good muscle growth I think I'll become too stocky and muscle-bound. Unfortunately, muscles I can control, height is another factor.

Graham, 19

Not particularly — that's why I work out.

David, 21

My feelings about my body change all the time. Sometimes I hate it, other times I'm reasonably content with it. It depends how much I've been drinking, eating and exercising. It's no work of art — but it does work.

Allan, 30

Happy. Everything's where it should be.

Liam, 29

Unhappy, and I get very pissed-off being continually reminded of it by magazines and TV showing the ideal as thin and fit.

Justin, 22

Who is? We're getting like women. Obsessed by our shape, fitness and looks. I've even heard that there are now male anorexics!

Hamish, 21

I'm too tall and too skinny — not enough meat.
Nick, 18

I've got bandy legs and a big arse — apart from that I'm perfect.

Gary, 22

I'm like a long streak of piss. And my legs are like string with knots in. Still, someone told me John Cleese was a sex symbol in America — so there's hope yet.
Kevin, 24

Most of the men claimed to be unhappy about their bodies and had considered them closely enough to be specific about what changes they'd like to make if it were possible.

WHICH PART OF YOUR BODY WOULD YOU SAY YOU WERE HAPPIEST ABOUT OR MOST PROUD OF?

Torso.

Vince, 19

Waist downwards.

Hamish, 21

Chest.

Andy, 25

Dick.

Darren, 19

My eyes and my smile seem kind of soft and seductive.

Julian, 19

My legs and my arms — biceps.

David, 21

My shoulders.

Chris, 18

My face. Women seem to like it.

Mark, 19

All of it, but especially my hands.

Jonathan, 21

None of it, although my penis gives me most pleasure.

Gary, 22

My legs, only because they attract the most compliments from women.

Philip, 20

*I was told I had 'nice buns' by two American girls.
This basically means buttocks, I believe. And I suppose
I can see what they mean. My bum is sort of small and
neat.*

Peter, 20

WHICH PART OF YOUR BODY ARE YOU LEAST HAPPY ABOUT AND WOULD MOST LIKE TO CHANGE?

My height, I'm 5ft 9in and I'd like to be 6ft.

Nick, 18

I'd like to stretch my legs a bit.

Andy, 25

*I wouldn't mind a couple of extra inches in the trouser
department.*

Robert, 19

*My rather large belly. I'm only about a stone and a
half overweight but it feels a lot more to me.*

Bryan, 28

*My arms are too skinny and my stomach's not flat
enough.*

Stephen, 18

My large stomach and my small pectorals.

Paul, 21

*Every time I look at a photograph of me, all I can see
is my arse. It looks like it's been stuck on as an
afterthought.*

Marcus, 23

*I could do with an extra few inches on my legs to
increase their length in proportion to the rest of my
body.*

Justin, 22

My face, but God knows how.

Mel, 23

My feet are too big but apart from that I'm happy.

Ian, 24

My skin. Having suffered from acne for over five years my face is a mess.

Peter, 20

My face is a mess. Sometimes I can't look people in the eye, especially girls, because it feels like they're just staring at my spots.

Gerry, 21

It's one thing to recognise that there are things about your body that you want to change, but it's another to actually get down and do something about it in terms of exercise or diet.

Fat seems to be just as much an issue with young men as it is with women. A great many boys and men write letters bemoaning the fact that they don't have a girlfriend 'because I'm too fat'.

They develop a negative image of themselves and can sound very bitter. Yet very few ever seem to mention dieting or schemes to lose weight. Unlike the girls who write, desperate for weight-loss solutions, the men seem much more resigned.

HAVE YOU EVER DIETED TO LOSE WEIGHT?

Yes, several times, but I keep on getting fat again.

Mark, 19

I have given up or cut down on the beer on a few occasions but that's about my limit.

Allan, 30

Yes, once I tried to cut down and lost 6lb in three weeks, but I need to have a lot of will-power and enthusiasm for it if I'm going to succeed.

Julian, 19

Yes. My mum went on the Cambridge diet and so I nicked some of her sachets. But they didn't do any good.

Richard, 20

No. I wouldn't really know how to. I know that things like chips are fattening, but what about stuff like meat and eggs?

Darren, 17

No. I'd get too hungry.

Morgan, 19

No. If I wanted to lose more weight I'd go to football training and running.

Darryl, 22

No, dieting's bad for you. It can make you bulimic.

Kajan, 18

No, I'm not that vain. I would like to be thinner because then I'd be right for my height, but I'd never go to Weight-Watchers or go on a diet, that's all faddy nonsense.

Andy, 25

WOULD YOU EVER CONSIDER HAVING COSMETIC SURGERY?

Yes, on my nose. It was broken in a rugby match, although I seem to be the only one who notices.

Kieran, 26

Yes, to remove a small scar from my nose which irritates me immensely.

Maurice, 18

I'd have a tattoo or a scar removed — if I had one.

Lewis, 24

I've got these really pronounced laughter lines at the side of my mouth. I'd like them smoothed out. I might go to a surgeon one day but I doubt it.

Jason, 25

Only if, through an accident, I became disfigured. Like that poor bastard Simon who was burnt in the Falklands.

Paul, 21

I wouldn't mind a collagen implant on my knob.

Vince, 19

No, we're made the way we are and knowing my luck I'd probably look worse afterwards anyway.

Robert, 19

No way, unless it was after some horrible accident. The risks of it going wrong so outweigh the possible benefits.

Aaron, 22

If I had an ugly great goiter that lived on the end of my nose then of course I'd have plastic surgery. But I wouldn't have collagen implants or any of those stupid vanity things done.

Ian, 24

If your face is ugly then people aren't nice to you. It's a proven fact. So maybe you ought to have surgery.

Chris, 18

If I grew great double chins I'd have them taken off because they make men look really old and fat.

Nick, 18

My nose is fat and blobby. I'd love a little nose. One without craters.

Paul, 21

People take the piss out of Michael Jackson but it's his *face. He can do what he wants. He can decorate his house all wacky, live with a chimp and no-one says anything, but as soon as he changes his face they make out he's a nutter. It doesn't make sense. Surely we have the right to choose what to do with our bodies. Mine's all right at the moment, but if I wasn't happy with it, I'd like to feel I was allowed to do whatever I liked to sort it, without being judged.*

Lewis, 18

No, but I think it's different for women. If you want bigger muscles you can go down the gym, but a woman can't just build bigger breasts, can she.

David, 21

So, the general consensus of opinion is that if you have some horrible disfigurement or medical complaint, then cosmetic surgery is permissible to put it right, but to have surgery purely for the sake of vanity, just to improve your looks, is not on.

There is, however, one part of the body that many men would like to be able to change:

THE PENIS

A man's penis becomes an issue from a very early age. The changing room or showers of secondary school are normally the first breeding grounds for complexes and insecurities about the dimensions of one's dick.

It's such an unfortunate member. It hangs between your legs on full display for your fellow, ferociously cruel school-mates to comment upon. It's supposed to be your symbol of manhood and tool for implementing sex, so if Ronnie Spriggs in the First Year says you've got a 'pygmy dick', it can be a very hard illusion to shake off.

I get a lot of letters from worried teenagers who think that their penises are going to be too small to have successful sex or make a girl happy. Their greatest fear is that they will attempt to have sex with a girl, fail, she will laugh and then tell all his mates. It's as though the most feared source of ridicule is the male peer group, but that the ridicule will result from an unsuccessful and therefore 'unmanly' experience with the opposite sex.

As a rule the penis issue gets easier as men grow older and come to terms with the fact that what they've got isn't going to get any bigger. But that doesn't mean the feelings of insecurity, envy and doubt go away entirely.

WOULD YOU SAY YOU WERE GENERALLY HAPPY ABOUT THE SIZE OF YOUR PENIS?

I am in general happy with my penis though at times I wonder whether women would get more pleasure if it was wider.

Mark, 19

I love the size of my penis. It is big. I know because I've compared it amongst friends.

Jonathan, 21

No, I would like it a bit bigger, but my girlfriend says she likes it the way it is.

Richard, 20

It is big and I'm not embarrassed at it at all.

Sean, 25

It could be a bit bigger but I've never had anyone comment on it being too small.

Paul, 21

I'm generally happy but have you ever met anyone who thought their penis was too big?

Kevin, 24

I've measured my penis and it is below average length by at least three or four centimetres. This worries me a lot. I don't want to be unsatisfactory at sex.

Pat, 17

The size of it is OK, but not brilliant. But it's the look that worries me. It looks so old and so oddly coloured. It is healthy though.

Kapil, 20

It's no truncheon but it gets me by.

Simon, 23

The overall impression was that most men rather begrudgingly accepted that they had sufficient size. Some revelled in their penis's superiority while others genuinely voiced concern that their tackle was going to cause them trouble.

Given that sex and women's pleasure are at the nub of the penis-size issue, you might expect that women were also responsible for sowing the seeds of doubt and insecurity.

HAS A WOMAN EVER COMMENTED ON THE SIZE OF YOUR PENIS?

Yes, she said it was a funny shape — much wider at the top than at the base.

Julian, 19

Yes, she said it was the biggest she had ever seen.

Vince, 19

My girlfriends have told me that I'm average. I think I'm small. Other men's cocks always look bigger.

Steven, 23

Not directly about its size, only complimentary things about how nice it looks.

Hamish, 21

My girlfriend's opinion will vary depending on how she feels. She'll say nice things about it when she wants something and be scathing when she wants to put me down.

Mel, 23

No, but I have heard her and one of her mates joking about the size of another boy's penis. They had a big laugh over it which really worried me. I got to thinking — do they say this about me *when I'm not here?*

Graham, 19

So, although men's worries about their penises stem from a fear of being inadequate sexually and laughed at by their peers, it seems that women themselves are not directly the cause of these fears.

Most seem to have derived encouragement and confidence from their personal encounters with women. However, peer pressure or peer fear seems to keep the 'worry level' high.

It is apparent from these interviews that men are as much a mass of insecurities as women. Men have done an excellent job of hiding these, from others as well as from themselves. It is only in the past few years they have started discussing them more openly.

Chapter Four

WHAT MEN THINK OF WOMEN

It's very difficult to get a lot of men to talk about women, on any level other than the physical one. They can tell you very quickly and graphically what they like and don't like about women's bodies, looks, clothes and behaviour. But defining 'personality' or describing the dynamics of an inter-personal relationship with a woman is something a lot of blokes just won't do.

Or if they do try, the results are often weak or incomprehensible. *'It means she's a good laugh'* and *'Doesn't take herself too seriously'* — were two of the most frequent phrases that came up on the subject of what makes a good personality.

Men don't talk to each other about women nearly as much as women might think they do. And they don't talk about women anything like as much as women talk about men. When men do talk to each other about women, they're usually at ease doing a bit of physical appraisal and comparison but tend to steer clear of discussing anything deeper.

It's often easier for a man to talk to another man about a totally unknown woman who walks past on the street than about a mutual female friend or a lover. It's far easier to turn to your best mate and say — *God, don't you just love the legs on her!* rather than — *My girlfriend keeps bursting into tears and I don't know what to do.*

Men don't make it easy for each other to go deeper into their feelings about anything much, especially when it's an area so tense and fraught with doubts as women.

One way of beginning to get an impression of what men think of women is to look at what they perceive as the differences between themselves and the opposite sex.

WHAT ARE THE MOST IMPORTANT DIFFERENCES BETWEEN MEN AND WOMEN?

A lot of men regard the difference as being enormous.

Women are soft and vulnerable. Men are hard.

Carl, 18

Women are into nest-building. Men are into their careers.

Philip, 20

Men have to know how to earn money and do stuff to keep paying rent and things. Women just have to know how to do cooking and shopping and bring up kids.

Ryan, 18

Men earn money — women spend money.

John, 24

Men are practical and logical — women are illogical and emotional.

Lewis, 24

Girls get all hot about green issues and seals. Men worry about Arsenal.

Vince, 19

Women take more care. They care about things. Men don't seem to care about much. Or if they do, they don't ever show it.

Julian, 19

Men are the best strategists. They think big, they plan and invent. Women have a tendency to see things on a smaller scale and think about details.

Gary, 22

Men take things. Women make things.

Scott, 20

Women are more understanding and have more to say. Men are too predictable, ie. sex, drink and girls.
Jeff, 28

Women are creative. Men are destructive. It's nurses versus soldiers.

Martin, 22

Other men painted the dividing line as being much fainter:

Nowadays there is no difference. Women can do everything that a man does and usually better.

Angus, 19

The Women's Movement has given women the power and opportunity to compete on all levels with men. They have equality.

Kieran, 26

Some men seemed to doggedly cling to a sense of superiority:

However much the Feminist Movement tries to deny it, men are still stronger than women. At the end of the day this physical superiority influences the way men and women interact.

Antonio, 23

Man and men are the leaders, the doers. Women have to prove themselves against a male standard. There's no doubt that they can do some things as well as us, but we invented *all the things they want to be good at.*
Richard, 20

Others readily admitted to feeling inferior:

We need women to have babies and make another generation, but women don't need us any more because they've got sperm banks.

Vince, 19

Men view life from a different perspective and men take advantage of women. Men think that they are the superior sex but women actually are.

Morgan, 19

Most men identified the major difference to be women's abilities to have babies and be emotionally caring. However, many thought that these differences hindered and weakened women:

My sister gets all tearful and upset when she sees things on the TV about starving people or babies in Romania. I know that it's sad and that, but it doesn't really affect me. I can look at it and I think . . . well, I don't think anything, because I know I can't do *anything.*

Maurice, 19

Women always seem to look to the future and want to know what's going to happen, especially in relationships. Whereas men can take it day by day and just let things happen if they do. But women always have to say things like 'I want to know where this relationship is going'. It can drive you mad.

Carl, 18

Two notions which appeared to be prevalent amongst respondents were that women have a wider view of the world and that they think most men are bastards. Some men felt this was very unfair, most seem to accept it with a sort of smug pride.

This brings into focus a question that I get asked very regularly by females who write to me – *Are men only interested in one thing?*

DO MEN ONLY THINK OF WOMEN IN TERMS OF THEIR SEXUALITY?

I know, from the hundreds of letters I've received from young men, that an awful lot of them do feel a great need to experience emotional relationships that are purely to do with togetherness and intimacy, not specifically to do with sex. But this non-sexual desire is something they express almost with a sense of embarrassment.

One way men avoid digging too deeply into their uncomfortable and uncharted emotional needs is to concentrate on their physical and visual preferences regarding women.

Once you get them started, it soon becomes clear that although they don't communicate a great deal, they have spent a lot of time thinking about specific physical likes and dislikes in great detail:

WHAT DO YOU FIND MOST PHYSICALLY ATTRACTIVE IN A WOMAN? AND WHICH CELEBRITY REPRESENTS YOUR IDEAL?

A certain proportion of the men automatically read physical to mean sexual:

> *A toned body is essential — beautiful legs, well defined abdominals and well-proportioned breasts, topped by large dark nipples. I find Lisa Bonet and Madonna's bodies the epitome of the word beautiful. However without doubt my ideal 'lady' would be Princess Diana.*
>
> Jonathan, 21

> *Legs and bum. I don't care so much about any other feature but a well proportioned bum is a great turn-on. Like Claudia Schiffer.*
>
> Nick, 18

I know it's a cliché but I think blonde women are much more attractive than brunettes. I don't know why but I believe it's more than just conditioning – they're genuinely sexier. My ideal is Michelle Pfeiffer.

Richard, 20

Long hair is always a turn-on for me. I like to think of what girls look like when they're naked with long, flowing hair.

Graham, 19

I don't like beanpole model figures. What I really like are curvy, sexy girls with a proper bust.

David, 21

Erect nipples in the summer.

Paul, 21

Long legs up to her armpits.

Lewis, 18

Really tanned bodies.

Adam, 19

Young girls are more attractive because they're fresher and have firmer bodies.

Michael, 25

I like girls with really smooth legs but I also like it when they've got golden down on their thighs too.

Chris, 18

Without a shadow of a doubt, Michelle Pfeiffer was most regularly cited as the ideal woman. Her slim, blonde looks and seductive temptress-like film roles have gained her pride of place in young men's fantasies.

But some men seemed to interpret 'physically attractive' as beauty rather than just raw sex:

I think Naomi Campbell is the world's most beautiful woman.

Bryan, 28

Girls with dark eyes that look a bit sad.

Sean, 25

Imam is the most attractive woman alive. Although   I am white I find black and mixed race women the most appealing.

Ian, 24

Face and head. My ideal is Sherilyn Fenn because she has great looks and physique whilst also a sultry and mysterious air.

Julian, 19

It's difficult to isolate individual features. I tend to look at a woman as a whole — so I suppose a fit body with long legs, but most important is her face, particularly the eyes.

Kevin, 24

And in terms of specific features, lips were very popular.

Some women's lips are enough on their own. It's almost as though the rest of the body doesn't matter. Look at Amanda de Cadenet.

Darryl, 22

Their lips, size and shape. The celebrity who represents my ideal woman is Michelle Pfeiffer.

Angus, 19

Other specific features included:

Eyes that engage you.

Frank, 24

Long, clean finger-nails.

Amin, 23

Clean-faced girls that don't wear loads of make-up.

Robert, 19

And one man resented the pressure he felt put under to like certain types:

I get annoyed at the way we are fed the ideal-shaped woman by the media. I think women are physically attractive in different ways, for example big breasts might look great on one girl but totally out of place on another. I suppose I prefer someone who doesn't fit the stereotype but that doesn't mean they should have a wooden leg or no teeth.

Marcus, 23

Once started, men may be quick to point out the positive physical attributes they like in women, but they're also keen to be specific about the things they don't like:

WHAT PHYSICAL ATTRIBUTES DO YOU FIND OFF-PUTTING?

As a lot of girls might fear, there is a certain proportion of men who latch on to weight-related things:

Cellulite, a large bum and gigantic breasts.

David, 21

Very overweight or skinny girls — anything too extreme.

Graham, 19

Sagging flesh.

Jeff, 28

Double chins.

Kieran, 26

A fat, low arse is a total passion killer.

Vince, 19

For some men weight wasn't a problem at all:

Fashion magazines are full of really bony models and lots of girls follow the example and get very, very thin. There's absolutely nothing wrong with having some curves and even some fat. Personally, I think it's preferable.

Julian, 19

Too skinny is unattractive. Girls should have meat in the right places.

Lee, 22

Being overweight wasn't really a major area of criticism though. It seemed to be either a lack of femininity or 'weirdness' that put men off:

Any excess facial or body hair. I don't know why but hairy legs, moustaches and stubbly armpits turn me right off.

Allan, 30

Fat is the thing with me. I'm not keen on fat girls.

Liam, 29

A lot of girls seem to want to look like boys these days and I find it a real no-no. I want girls to look feminine and attractive. That doesn't mean I'm a chauvinist or anything, I just think it looks better.   It would be a weird world if we all looked the same.

Tim, 20

I hate girls with tattoos.

Antonio, 23

Those nose-rings that girls wear are ridiculous. You don't know whether to chat them up or lead them to a milking stall.

Lewis, 24

I hate hairy women — hairy legs or facial hair is repulsive.

Adam, 19

Small tits are no fun — you might as well go out with a bloke!

Nick, 18

Girls with moustaches.

Graham, 19

Hard looking girls with stares that go right through you.

Maurice, 18

Dykey hair styles that are all short and spikey.

Colin, 22

Thin lips.

Kapil, 20

Very short hair, bad breath and open facial zits. But I don't actually find much about women off-putting. I look at most people as who they are, not what they are.

Mark, 19

One girl I went out with had a big hairy mole on her lip. I couldn't kiss her 'cause of it.

Jeff, 28

Women who obviously don't care about how they look. It shows a lot about a woman's personality.

Marcus, 23

Although men obviously like women to be feminine, most seem to favour a 'natural' look, reacting against women who try too hard.

Too much make-up is bad news. It's evidence that's she's obviously trying too hard, got something to hide or really is a dog.

Darryl, 22

Stick-on, false fingernails covered in lurid varnish.

Sam, 24

Anything artificial — like too much make-up or dyed hair, but worst of all is obvious plastic surgery — an old face stretched over an old head looks revolting.

Jason, 25

Height was an issue with a few:

Very tall women — but that's probably because I'm only 5' 5".

Aaron, 22

And finally, so was 'bad personality' as portrayed by appearance:

Girls who look like they've got a lemon stuck up their arse and never smile.

Kevin, 24

Men's thoughts about women's behaviour are much more revealing in terms of what they do and don't like about a woman's personality:

WHAT SORT OF BEHAVIOUR DO YOU FIND ATTRACTIVE IN A WOMAN?

A sense of contrast or even contradiction scored high:

Intelligence and wit with a slight bit of naivety.

Gerry, 26

Intelligence and a good easy sense of humour plus courteous manners and honesty.

Richard, 20

Being able to laugh and not get too serious, but still be sensitive.

Adam, 19

Generosity, kindness, expressing sexuality, being dominant in a relationship. A kind of shyness but an inner confidence.

Morgan, 19

So did a sense of humour . . .

Someone who can take a joke.

Jeremy, 24

Who doesn't mind mucking about with the lads and having a laugh. Doesn't always want attention and stuff.

Nick, 18

. . . or a lack of humour:

One girl I went with used to get the hump with me over any little thing. She was a real looker but far too moody.

Keith, 18

I like birds that smile. Stuck-up, hoity-toity ones are a waste of space.

Graham, 19

So did a sense of sexy flirtatiousness:

Girls who are good in bed.

Mark, 19

Sexual behaviour.

Darren, 19

Flirty girls who play up to you.

John, 24

Although not for every man:

I detest flirtatious women — she has to be cultured, stylish and elegant but at the same time modest.

Hamish, 21

Men are definitely concerned as well with how a woman perceives them:

There are so many women who look at you as though you are some sort of worm. I often find that men get

judged together and some women look at you as if
you've just wolf-whistled or leered at them. But we are
all different. I don't leer at women. So I like women
that look at me with respect.

Neil, 22

I like women who are interested in the things
I've got to say. Too often I find that women are
incomprehensible. I don't understand the sometimes
conflicting messages that they put out. I like women
who are clear and straightforward without all that
game-playing.

Marcus, 23

How women reacted to and with men could also be a
major turn-off:

WHAT SORT OF BEHAVIOUR DO YOU FIND OFF-PUTTING?

Men don't like to think that they are being taken for a ride,
and they want to be thought about.

Girls that giggle and talk with each other when you
walk into the room. It's like you imagine they're
talking about you but they don't talk to you.

Pat, 19

Girls that wind you up and say that they fancy you or
that one of their mates fancies you — but they don't
really. They just do it to get a reaction.

Jeremy, 24

Women who are self-obsessed.

Tom, 21

At the same time, too blatant a show of affection is seen
by some as a bad thing:

Women who get too serious, too soon.

Tim, 20

Ones that keep wanting you to say 'I love you'.

Gerry, 26

Girlfriends that paw you and hug you and want you to kiss them when all your mates or their mates are sitting about watching.

Angus, 19

Kissing in public.

Chris, 24

Insecurity — women who are never sure where they stand in a relationship and always need reassuring. It gets to the pitch where you are spending your whole time keeping them happy and you never have any time to just relax and enjoy the relationship. It just wears you down.

Philip, 20

Possessiveness — I hate it when she starts to treat you like her property, always wanting to know where you've been, who you've seen and what you've been up to. You need a bit of trust and your own space in a relationship to make it work.

Graham, 19

Some men found 'unfeminine' behaviour a big problem:

A foul mouth, promiscuity, smoking.

Bryan, 28

Drinking out of a pint pot and behaving like a 'girl' — you know, lots of screaming and hugging.

Mark, 19

Girls that fart and think it's funny.

Victor, 17

Smoking is a real turn-off for me. I can just imagine what her mouth would taste like — an old ashtray.

Keith, 18

Women who won't stop talking.

Justin, 22

Smoking, swearing, bitchiness and back-stabbing. And of course vanity.

Richard, 20

Loud women who talk before they think.

Peter, 20

Drunk women who get all sloppy and messy.

Danny, 19

Men are frightened or angered by what seems to be a contradiction. They don't like being led on.

Women who say one thing and mean another.

Aaron, 22

Women who tease you just for the sake of proving they can.

Tom, 21

Prick-teasers.

Pat, 19

When she gives out signals that make you think that she really likes you, then goes and does something to make you feel stupid — like tell her mates about you.

Ryan, 18

What men think of as off-putting behaviour includes other areas:

I hate that business that some women do where they have to turn every little thing into a massive crisis. Drama queens.

Michael, 25

Blatant narrow-mindedness, making any judgments in situations which are unreal. Snobbery and being two-faced.

Stephen, 18

And to some men, behaviour is only a manifestation of something more important:

Surely a woman's behaviour is only a reflection of her personality. You either love a woman for her personality or you don't. It shouldn't and can't be modified to suit.

Mark, 19

A general admiration for women is something most seem to agree about. A lot of men seemed to zero in on the physical differences between the sexes and marvel at women's reproductive functions and physical grace:

WHAT DO YOU FIND ADMIRABLE ABOUT WOMEN?

I think being able to stay alive while giving birth is very admirable.

Paul, 21

Their ability to have babies.

Justin, 22

How they put up with all the shit men give them. And all the things they live with and have to do that men don't . . . eg. sexism, small-mindedness, periods and pregnancy.

Kieran, 26

Putting up with periods every month must be difficult but I suppose they've got no choice.

Simon, 23

Elegance and grace and an innate sense of rhythm which all women seem to possess.

Julian, 19

The way they move.

Morgan, 19

Women's unity was another source of admiration:

The way they can talk to each other about anything.
Chris, 18

Men always seem to be waiting to take the piss out of each other whereas girls are a support and a good influence to their friends.
Julian, 19

And even their sheer difference from men was seen as a plus:

It often seems to me that women are a completely different breed from men. Their approach to life is much more realistic and honest. They don't seem to be consumed in petty conquests and posturing like so many men are. They don't involve themselves with the same sort of breast-beating and showing-off. They are more content to get on with each other.
Michael, 25

The seemingly admirable mixture of sexiness, child-bearing abilities, intellectual and emotional understanding is apparent in the range of men's ideal, fantasy partner:

DESCRIBE YOUR IDEAL GIRLFRIEND/WIFE?

Intelligent, impeccably well-dressed and mannered, successful, healthy, tall, cultured and possessing a ferocious sense of humour – no more than usual!
Jonathan, 21

Winona Ryder.
Angus, 19

Beautiful, rich, kind and blonde.
Stephen, 18

Julia Roberts.
Ryan, 18

*For a wife I'd like Princess Diana, but for my
girlfriend I'd like Madonna.*

David, 21

A good mother for my children.

Amin, 23

Someone who understands me.

Jeremy, 24

Someone who really got on with my mates.

Victor, 19

*I think my ideal changes from week to week.
The more girls I see and the more I meet, the more
different ones I want.*

Richard, 20

*Someone who is not afraid to speak her mind and be
her own woman.*

Mel, 23

*Quite chatty and friendly, shows her emotions and
withholds none. Quite physical and thoughtful.
Physically she'd be about my height, average weight
and beautiful lips.*

Danny, 19

*My ideal girlfriend doesn't exist. In real life you'll
never find someone with all the qualities you think
you want but that doesn't mean you can't find
someone to love and who will love you.*

Sean, 20

A cross between Felicity Kendall and Dannii Minogue.
Robert, 19

So most men admit they admire women and regard
them with a certain amount of respect and awe. On the
whole they prefer unthreatening women and are more
attracted to feminine or quietly sexy ones. Does this mean
that they are scared of certain types of women?

WOULD YOU CONSIDER YOURSELF IN ANY WAY SCARED OF WOMEN?

Some men are adamant they have no fear:

No, not at all.

Kapil, 20

No. Why should I be? They are only people like us.

Julian, 19

Others admit to being selectively worried:

No, not in general, but there is a type of woman which I find frightening. Usually quite tall and hard-looking with a fierce look about them and although they can be quite attractive you can imagine they could easily get vicious if you didn't meet with their expectations.

Frank, 24

Not in a physical way – but a woman like Sharon Stone or Sandra Bernhard would be quite daunting to take to bed. You might get hurt . . . emotionally that is, rather than physical damage.

Martin, 22

I'm kind of scared of tall women. I always think they hate me.

Morgan, 19

With some it's not so much individuals as numbers:

I don't find women individually scary – well sometimes, but when they are in a cohesive group and they're being loud or aggressive I can't deal with them.

Lee, 22

And for many more men it is not women themselves that scare them, but what they think women represent:

> *I'm not scared of women, but I'm scared of their expectations, particularly when it comes to sex.*
>
> Robert, 19

> *Yes, of how they can upset you, rip you off, in fact ruin your life. But that's mainly up to you.*
>
> Darren, 19

> *Women's anger scares me. They show it so readily and so powerfully. Men simmer and sulk more. I understand men so I know what to expect. Women still frighten me because they're unpredictable.*
>
> Alex, 22

> *If a woman gets her claws into you, you ought to be scared. If you're not — you've got a screw loose somewhere.*
>
> Pat, 19

> *Who do you think I am . . . Jason Donovan?*
>
> Richard, 20

A fear of women can be purely a fear of the unknown and the unfathomable, or it may be fear triggered by a sense of inferiority. A fear of women can stem from having a powerful mother. Some of the men who spoke of their admiration for women, did so with such a tone of reverence, particularly with regard to their child-bearing abilities, suggesting that they themselves may have felt grossly inferior in comparison.

IN WHAT WAYS ARE MEN BETTER THAN WOMEN?

Strength scored high:

> *I believe physical strength leads to strength in the mind, therefore men are more resilient and possess   a stronger will.*
>
> Hamish, 21

Aggression, physical exertion, practical applications.

Vince, 19

Just physical strength; women aren't more stupid or anything but just weaker, and I happen to be the opposite sex.

Andy, 25

Men are better at aggressive activities — like starting wars.

Aaron, 22

So did emotional control:

Men are better survivors. Women take things too seriously and let things cripple them.

Angus, 19

Men keep a grip at times when women tend to go to pieces. In disasters and accidents for example.

Jeremy, 24

The attributes that some men praised women for, like being more emotionally open and caring, were the same characteristics that made other men criticise them.

IN WHAT WAYS ARE WOMEN BETTER THAN MEN?

On the whole they have stacks more common sense than men. They are more sensitive to people and the needs of those around them. You can rely on them.

Justin, 22

They're more flexible.

Jeff, 28

They're more concerned about friendships, love and the feelings of others.

Paul, 21

They're not better, just different.

Alex, 22

They are better at expressing themselves and letting you know what they really want.

Julian, 19

Women are more intuitive. Men are analytical.

Colin, 22

Women don't get hung up on stupid stuff like men.

Pat, 19

They're more selfish and better at not succumbing to peer pressure.

Raj, 21

Women are better liars than men. Men lie more often but women do it better.

Mel, 23

One thing that quickly becomes apparent when you ask men about their views on women is how contradictory they can be. Some men admire women's abilities to deal with their feelings and express their emotions openly, whereas other men abhor what they see as this sort of out-of-control, over-emotional, drama-queen syndrome. We've already seen that the men interviewed would talk to a female if they had an emotional crisis in their life.

There is a mass of double standards surrounding how a woman should appear and behave. The joke about wanting a woman to be a 'wife in the kitchen and a whore in the bedroom' is not that far from the truth.

Chapter Five

RELATIONSHIPS WITH WOMEN

From the quotes in Chapter 4, What Men Think Of Women, it's apparent that many men spend a fair amount of time considering what they like and don't like about women. They have well-developed ideas on how they like a woman to look and act. But this doesn't mean that they necessarily analyse what it is that they want from a relationship with a woman.

Some stated that having a beautiful girlfriend can give a man a certain amount of enviable kudos and admiration amongst his peer group. But what about love and emotion? How do they rate these?

HOW IMPORTANT IS YOUR LOVE LIFE COMPARED WITH OTHER ASPECTS OF YOUR LIFE?

Most felt it was of prime significance:

Very important. I don't feel my life is complete unless it includes a good relationship.

Julian, 19

Crucial. Everything else pales by comparison.

Ian, 24

I've never really rated it in terms of importance because I feel it is an essential part of life . . . I'm never out of a relationship.

Bryan, 28

Others saw it only as a balanced equal part:

It's as important as anything else — like work or friends.

Richard, 20

More important than friends, less important than football.

Gary, 22

It's on a par with work and my social life.

Mark, 19

It's nice to have a love life but I wouldn't say it was the be-all and end-all. There are more important things in my life.

Sean, 20

Some mourned its absence:

It hardly exists so I suppose its absence is quite important!

Mel, 23

I don't know what being in love means.

Pat, 19

Being in love is obviously good when it happens. But no-one should feel incomplete if they are not in love. It's far more important to be your own man and be at ease with who you are, not who you love.

Angus, 19

I don't know. I don't think I've ever been in love.

Scott, 20

No-one slagged it off as irrelevant or bad news.
Everyone seemed to regard love with a sense of respect.

The whole notion of being in love is a very esoteric and personal state. And everyone has their own definition.

WHAT DOES BEING 'IN LOVE' MEAN TO YOU?

Wanting to be with someone all the time; having a desire to touch and hold them when they are next to you; feeling elated in their presence and hollow when they are gone.

Julian, 19

Loving everything about someone and looking forward to what you have together. It's totally overwhelming and overrides any other emotion.

Robert, 19

Having someone just as important as yourself in your life.

Chris, 24

Feeling at one with the world.

Paul, 21

It's like wanting to run and scream and shout and hug and hide all at the same time.

Maurice, 18

Knowing someone else is really there for you.

Adam, 19

It's about trusting and caring and forgiving.

Graham, 19

Being totally in tune with another person.

Marcus, 23

Imminent disaster.

Antonio, 23

Not a lot.

Michael, 25

Never having been there I don't think I know.

Scott, 20

Part of the fear of love expressed by some was about losing control of their otherwise tightly-leashed emotions.

One of the most regular problems I come across in letters men write to me involves a sense of confusion over how many women they can love at one time. They are often seeing two women and are convinced they are in love with them both and don't know what to do.

Some men **have great difficulty** expressing their emotions and **showing** their love, whereas others find themselves **in a quandary** of going out with two women simultaneously.

DO YOU THINK YOU CAN BE IN LOVE WITH MORE THAN ONE WOMAN AT THE SAME TIME?

A few were adamant that it was impossible:

Definitely not. I tried it — it does your head in.

Darryl, 22

No, real love is all-consuming and indivisible.

Peter, 20

No. If you really are in love with one woman you couldn't hurt her by even thinking of another.

Stephen, 18

Most thought it was possible, although not practical:

Yes, if you can cope with it in your own head. But then you've got to cope with it practically too.

Jeff, 28

Yes in theory, but no in practice.

Nick, 18

Yes, but I wouldn't want to try it. It's too dangerous!

Peter, 20

It's a very old-fashioned idea that you can only be in love with one person at a time. On several occasions I have had more than one girlfriend and can honestly say that I have been in love with both of them.

Neil, 22

Why not?

Angus, 19

Well yes, but you can't tell a woman that you're in love with someone else too because they wouldn't understand — would they?

Justin, 22

It's not a situation that any woman I know has been willing to accept. But then I doubt I could handle a relationship with a woman who was going out with another man.

Martin, 22

The general consensus regarding going out with two women seemed to be that it was acceptable if it could be engineered. The attitude of some men to monogamy was strangely different.

DO YOU BELIEVE IN MONOGAMY?

If it's a serious relationship, it's got to be monogamous otherwise it's dangerous.

Chris, 18

Yes, for two people who are getting married and want to have children.

Peter, 20

I think I do. I think I'd like to be in a monogamous relationship but I've never met anyone I like enough.

Simon, 23

Yes. Monogamy is better for you. It's safer sex.

Adam, 19

I believe in it. I just don't necessarily practise it. Though I'm not saying I wouldn't. It's just I don't.

Michael, 25

Totally. Trust and dependency make a marriage. Duplicity destroys it.

Frank, 24

Sexual duplicity, being unfaithful to your partner, is one way of destroying a relationship. It's also something that a lot of men seem to have experienced first-hand.

HAVE YOU EVER BEEN UNFAITHFUL TO A GIRLFRIEND OR WIFE? WAS IT AN EASY DECISION TO MAKE AND HOW DID YOU FEEL ABOUT YOUR BEHAVIOUR?

Yes, once. The decision was easy to make but I'll always regret it. It caused the break-up of my marriage which was worth a lot more than the affair.
Neil, 22

Yes, but it filled me with guilt – it just wasn't worth it.
David, 21

Yes, and it was surprisingly easy to do. I was consumed with guilt but decided not to tell my girlfriend. We've since split up but I still haven't told her. In future I think it would be a much more difficult and considered decision but I suppose I can't rule it out. Men are built like that – if it's offered on a plate then they'll take it.

Simon, 23

Yes, but as my wife was having an affair at the time it was a fairly easy decision to make. I'm no longer married, by the way.

Sean, 25

Yes and yes. And I hope you're asking some women this question.

Mel, 23

Yes. I wish I could say it was something I considered carefully, but I didn't. A situation just arose and I reacted to it. Then it all became an unholy mess.
Alex, 22

Yes, it was a one-off fling which didn't mean anything. I felt a small twinge of guilt but if anything it had a positive effect on my relationship with my girlfriend.

Julian, 19

Yes, I couldn't resist, she was beautiful and begging for it.

Nick, 18

Yes, once. I felt like an adulterer – mean and unfaithful. It made me look very closely at myself.

Marcus, 23

Yes. Dead easy.

Lee, 22

Yes, I'm having one at the moment and my girlfriend doesn't know. Although the 'other woman' knows about my girlfriend and says she doesn't care.

Colin, 22

Far fewer men resisted temptation:

No, I would never be unfaithful as this would be an irrevocable destruction of trust and this is essential in any relationship.

Angus, 19

No, I will always finish one relationship before starting another one.

Amin, 23

No, I believe in 'do unto others' and I would be pole-axed if she did it to me.

Steve, 23

No, but I suppose I couldn't rule it out.

Richard, 20

Not really. Well I kissed another girl once, but God I felt guilty.

Jeremy, 24

The guilt that men felt after being unfaithful affected their relationship in one way or another.

WHAT WAS THE EFFECT ON THE RELATIONSHIP?

Most men interviewed continued to keep it a secret.

I didn't tell her, so things carried on as normal for a bit, but I think it was the beginning of the end for our relationship. We split up about six months later.

David, 21

None, she doesn't know — thank God. I don't like keeping it from her but I value our relationship more than this one kiss.

Jeremy, 24

It carried on as normal.

Philip, 20

What the mind doesn't know the heart doesn't grieve about.

Lee, 22

Others felt a need to confess:

In a fit of guilt-ridden anxiety I came clean. We didn't split up but it caused a hell of a bad few weeks. Looking back I think I'd have been better to keep my mouth shut.

Simon, 23

She left me but I think it was going to happen anyway.

David, 21

She was initially very upset but after a lot of talking and apologising on my part we are still together. I still don't think she's forgiven me though.

Alex, 22

Some were discovered:

She did find out because someone else told her. Now she's quite suspicious and asks me a lot of boring questions.

Mel, 25

She found a letter and confronted me. After the initial upset and tears, it made me think how grateful I was for the relationship I had, and still have, with my wife.

Marcus, 23

Some men have dishonest or certainly unreal relationships with their close friends. Generally, they seem to be more open and honest with women.

DO YOU THINK YOU ARE MORE OR LESS HONEST WITH YOUR MALE FRIENDS THAN YOU ARE WITH YOUR GIRLFRIEND OR WIFE?

The majority said they were more honest to women:

I am more honest with my girlfriend. With male friends there is always a temptation to embellish stories to make your life more exciting.

Mark, 19

Definitely more honest with women. They are much easier to talk to and there's no need for macho bullshit.

Gary, 22

I'm definitely more honest with women because I feel a pressure to have to keep face with my mates. I can be vulnerable and down in front of women.

Frank, 24

A few cited the sanctity of male friendship:

I'm more honest with my mates because they understand me better. If I told them I was up to no good they'd not judge me, but a girl might .

Danny, 19

I wouldn't lie to my mates. Friendship is everything.

Victor, 19

I can envisage two-timing a girlfriend, but not a mate. I mean you can't in the same way anyway. But a mate would know the truth about me. A girlfriend would only see what I wanted her to see.

Nick, 18

Others stated that they had no allegiances:

Neither. I am dishonest with both in certain situations.

Sean, 20

Whenever I'm dishonest, it's for a good reason. The reasons change depending on who it is. I don't set out to be dishonest to either sex, but I am sometimes.

Bryan, 28

It'll come as no revelation to any women that men can be enormously dishonest. They can be dishonest in relationships, dishonest with each other and dishonest with themselves. Sometimes they can even be dishonest because they think it's the right thing to do.

Dishonesty to women can take the form of infidelity in relationships, lying about previous partners or even by just saying 'I love you' when in truth they definitely don't.

HAVE YOU EVER SAID 'I LOVE YOU' TO A WOMAN WHEN YOU KNOW THAT IT'S NOT TRUE?

Yes, so that I could have sex with her. She must have believed me because we had sex!

Richard, 20

Several times. It's what women expect of you.

Marcus, 23

Only once, and then it was more a case of not being sure. It was expedient at the time but as I went on to feel that I did love her I think it was OK.

John, 24

Only when I thought it'd do me good.

Keith, 18

Yes, because she kept asking me why I never said it. I could have said 'because I don't' – which would have hurt her, so I said 'I love you'.

Kieran, 26

Yes. I'm sure all men have said it when they don't mean it, or at least don't know it – either that or they're lying.

Ian, 24

Sure. It works wonders.

Vince, 19

Most have lied about love in some respect. However, others were adamant how important it was to be truthful:

No. I don't feel I have to say things I don't mean.

Chris, 18

No. What's the point?

Steve, 23

No. If I lied to a girl about loving her I would in effect only be lying to myself. I owe myself better than that.

Aaron, 22

No. 'Love' is an over-used and abused term as it is.

Kevin, 24

No. I've never told any girl that I love her. Love is a myth.

Morgan, 19

Very often when men lie, it's not necessarily meant to be malicious or deceptive, but a way of 'protecting' women from the truth. It's as though some men believe that they know better than a woman what level of honesty is good for her.

HAVE YOU EVER LIED TO A WOMAN IN ORDER TO AVOID HURTING HER FEELINGS?

Yes, it's the right thing to do.

Angus, 19

Yes, I went out one evening and got very drunk resulting in me being sick seven times that night. I told my girlfriend I had 'flu but I later told her the truth as the guilt was too much.

Mark, 19

Yes, during an argument with my girlfriend she asked me whether I honestly thought she didn't love me.   I thought she didn't but I told her what she wanted to hear — that she did! I felt it was the right thing to do as she is very temperamental and if I'd told the truth she might have ignored me for days.

Peter, 20

Yes, because if she knew the whole truth about me — she'd hate me.

Sean, 24

*Yes. I was finishing a relationship because I didn't like
her but I said that I just wasn't ready for one!
I thought it was the right thing to do as there's no
point in hurting anyone's feelings if you can avoid it.*
Steven, 23

*I had a mini-fling with my girlfriend's best friend.   I
thought it was up to her (the friend) to tell her if she
wanted to. I didn't think it was my business. So I told
her I'd been seeing someone she didn't know.*
Sean, 20

*Yes, it was about how she looked, how she wasn't fat.
It was the right thing to say because she's so self-
conscious.*
Scott, 20

*Her sister is a slag who tried to get off with me at a
dance party when my girlfriend was ill. I never told
her the truth about what happened because it would
cause a family fight.*
Lewis, 18

Yes of course.
Jim, 20

In a way, some men are more sensitive on hurting their
partners than women. Men find it more difficult to say   'I
like you, but I don't love you'. They may lie but I have
found as they get older they tend to lie less about this sort
of thing. They resort usually to just saying nothing. This is
very safe.

Most men believed in 'lying for good reason', but not
all:

*No. It only serves to make things worse. No-one likes
being lied to, it makes you feel betrayed.*
Gerry, 26

No. Even if truth hurts it's for the best.
Michael, 25

No, and I hope I never do.

Martin, 22

The fact that some men assume they know when is the 'right' time to tell the truth and when it's better to lie, suggests they think they know what is 'best' for their partners. This would in turn suggest that they have an insight into women's needs within a relationship. So, are these needs vastly different from a man's needs?

Do You Think Women Want Different Things From A Relationship Than Men?

The majority of men recognised a difference:

Yes. In a proper relationship, women rightfully want attention, loyalty and respect, trust and love. Men tend to prefer material things, eg. sex.

Danny, 19

Yes, women want more emotional contact. Some men enter relationships purely for the physical side.

Nick, 18

Women want security, men want sex.

Tom, 21

Women tend to look at the longer-term aspects of a relationship almost before they've started it, while men tend to take things as they come. That's why so many men get frightened when girlfriends start to talk about marriage.

Neil, 22

Definitely, but I don't know what they are.

Pat, 19

Others were convinced that we are all basically after the same thing:

No, we all want someone to love us.

Julian, 19

*Not necessarily, both men and women enter
relationships with different (usually unstated) aims
and often no real ability to communicate. That's why
so many relationships don't last.*

Andy, 25

*It depends on each individual man and woman.
Sometimes it doesn't matter that they want different
things if their needs are compatible.*

Steve, 23

Most of the respondents felt that one of the essential
differences between men and women with regard to
relationships was that men were more content with a
physical and sexual relationship, whereas women wanted
to take things deeper to establish emotional ties.
Is sex such a big issue with men?

HOW IMPORTANT IS SEX IN YOUR RELATIONSHIPS WITH WOMEN?

*Making love, rather than sex, is a very important part
of my relationships. Sex involves one person whereas
making love involves two.*

Julian, 19

*Very important – it is the cornerstone of our
relationship. Without sex we wouldn't have a
relationship.*

Simon, 23

*It would be difficult to imagine my present
relationship without sex although in the past I have
been in a relationship where sex gradually became
less important – but that was the beginning of the
end.*

Mel, 23

It's the whole point!

Chris, 18

It's important, but not as important as the magazines and tabloids would have us believe.

John, 24

Easily the majority of men felt that sex was an essential part of an inter-personal relationship with a woman. But it is obvious that this actually only relates to a certain type of relationship, because many men felt that non-sexual friendships were possible and important too.

IS IT POSSIBLE TO HAVE PURELY PLATONIC RELATIONSHIPS WITH WOMEN? HOW DO THESE FRIENDSHIPS DIFFER FROM THOSE WITH YOUR MALE FRIENDS?

For many men it seems these friendships act as a sort of emotional life-line:

Yes, I find I'm more honest, more myself with girl friends.

Richard, 20

Yes. They're very different from my male friends because there's no rivalry.

Jonathan, 21

Yes. I have several women who are close friends. These friendships are less raucous and abusive than male relationships and centre on different things — less drinking and shouting.

Danny, 19

Yes. Platonic relationships with women are very important to me. They are different from both my relationships with my male friends and the sexual relationships with women. Women seem to understand more about emotional matters and not having sisters or a mother to talk to, it makes these relationships very valuable.

Chris, 24

They differ from my male friends in that with women we talk more about personal things. They give better advice and they generally take life more seriously.

Mark, 19

Yes, some of my best friends are women.

Bryan, 28

This does rather suggest that contrary to popular belief, a lot of men aren't 'only after one thing'.

For a small proportion though, there is a sense of doubt as to whether men and women can be just friends:

I would like to think so but I don't think it's possible. Whenever I've got close to a woman in what I thought was a platonic relationship it's turned out that she fancied me all along.

Hamish, 21

I'm not sure. Whenever you get close to a woman you end up wanting to sleep with her.

Steve, 23

I used to think so but it's a bit of a myth.

Paul, 21

No. All my female friends are either girlfriends, ex-girlfriends or prospective girlfriends.

Vince, 19

Even the girls that I've been friends with but not got off with, I've wanted to. I've hung around with them sometimes even though we're not going together just so my mates'll see me and think I'm 'in there'.

Morgan, 19

Whether or not men can have platonic relationships, they are certain they understand what women mean about being deep.

WOMEN OFTEN COMPLAIN THAT MEN ARE 'SHALLOW' RATHER THAN 'DEEP'. WHAT DO YOU THINK THEY MEAN AND DO YOU THINK YOU ARE A DEEP PERSON?

Deep means emotional. One whose emotions are a great part of their life. I would consider myself a deep person — one hour does not pass without me regarding my thoughts and fears on life and everything.

Vince, 19

I'd say I was deep. When women talk in such terms they are often referring to love. Deep suggests a caring nature with a willingness to commit oneself and understand things from the woman's perspective.

Paul, 21

Being called shallow is just a term of abuse comparable to insincere or unthinking.

Marcus, 23

Being deep means you're not trying to shag them on the first date — I think.

Gerry, 26

I'd like to think I was deep. Someone who's shallow is someone who's just into material things. Who's just in life for kicks and doesn't worry about more serious matters.

Jeremy, 24

Worrying about serious matters too much can also be an affliction. Being too serious or 'taking yourself too seriously' is often used as a put-down.

Most surveys concerning what women find attractive in men, show that a sense of humour is normally at or very near the top of the list. Yet when men are asked what they think makes them attractive, they usually put money and good looks first.

WHAT THINGS DO WOMEN FIND ATTRACTIVE IN MEN?

A good body and a good job.

Jonathan, 21

A lot of women fancy older men who've got money and a bit of class.

Julian, 19

Designer clothes, Italian car and his own apartment.

Maurice, 18

Women like men who are sensitive but strong, handsome but not vain, and self-assured.

Michael, 25

A guy who's not going to two-time them with every girl he meets and who wants a family and kids.

Darryl, 22

Money.

Kapil, 20

Someone like Lovejoy who is a bit of a lad but brainy as well.

Adam, 19

Own teeth, own hair, own car, own house.

Simon, 23

A man who will respect them and treat them as equals.

Robert, 19

If this is what men think women want, how do they feel about sexual 'rules'?

Some couples fall into bed together on their first night out and then continue to see each other and form a relationship, while others go through a courting period which sees a gradual increase in physical intimacy, culminating in sex.

Which do men prefer or expect, getting to know a woman then having sex, or having sex, then getting to know her?

DO YOU EXPECT A GIRL TO HAVE SEX WITH YOU ON THE FIRST DATE?

No.

Adam, 19

No, but I can live in hope — can't I?

Angus, 19

I certainly wouldn't expect it, but I wouldn't be horrified if it happened.

Sean, 20

No, and I wouldn't want to have sex with her. It's too soon. I'd feel too embarrassed being naked or anything in front of her.

David, 21

The first date is stretching it. Third or fourth maybe.
Tim, 20

Unless you already know the girl as a friend, the first date's not about sex, it's about finding out if you like each other.

Julian, 19

The golden rule is never expect something — because then it won't happen. Play it cool and who knows.
Colin, 22

The consensus of opinion was that to expect sex was going too far but that it was a welcome possibility. Some felt it was expected in certain situations.

It depends who it is. If she's classy then no. If she's someone you picked up in a club then yes — you'd be looking for an early night.

Lewis, 24

*I'd expect something. Maybe not 'the business', but
something to keep me interested. Otherwise what'd be
the point?*

Scott, 20

*If a girl didn't want to sleep with me then I wouldn't
want to go with her.*

Lee, 22

And if sex did occur on the first night, does that mean
that the men would make a value judgment about the girls'
character?

IF YOU HAD SEX WITH A GIRL ON THE FIRST DATE, WOULD YOU THINK SHE'S A SLAG?

Some men sat on the fence:

*I wouldn't say she was a slag exactly. But I would
wonder how many other blokes she'd done that with.*

Kapil, 20

*Not a slag, that's too strong. I'd think she was pretty
wild or else had fallen in love with me.*

Graham, 19

Others were protective:

*If she's a slag then I must be a slag too for doing it
with her.*

Julian, 19

*If that's what she wants to do then fine. I don't think
men should be critical about another individual's
choice of behaviour, man or woman.*

Philip, 20

And the minority were accusing:

*A woman who shags a total stranger is a slag — no
question.*

Brian, 21

Some men do claim to find women who are forward and sexually aggressive off-putting. They presumably feel threatened or emasculated in some way. Does this mean that men don't want to be pursued by women? Are men only happy if they are the pursuers?

HOW WOULD YOU FEEL IF A WOMAN ASKED YOU OUT? WOULD YOU MIND BEING CHASED?

All men who answered were in favour:

I'd love it if a woman asked me out. I'd think it was Christmas.

Gary, 22

I'd have absolutely no objections to being asked out by a woman. Being asked doesn't mean I have to accept — does it?

Steve, 23

Most of the girls I've been out with have asked me. I've only ever done the asking once or twice. To me it seems normal.

Jeremy, 24

I'd be flattered. It'd be a relief from trying to work up the courage to ask them out.

Peter, 20

I have been asked out, and even propositioned by women. It's exciting and not in the slightest bit threatening. Made me feel great.

Andy, 25

As long as she didn't make a spectacle of it, didn't show me up by going over the top, then I'd be into it.

Mark, 19

None of the respondents were worried or put off by the idea of a woman taking the initiative in starting a relationship. In fact, many had first hand experience of this happening. Particularly amongst the teenage respondents, the practice of girls asking boys out seemed to be almost standard and totally acceptable.

One of the most regularly cited reasons for being happy to have women do the asking was because in this situation the pressure is taken off the male risking rejection by doing the asking himself.

Fear of rejection is undoubtedly the single most common reason for not starting a relationship. I receive thousands of letters about being too scared to risk asking someone out. Both men and women suffer from the fear of rejection. Some men even named it as their greatest fear.

But what does rejection actually feel like to men?

HOW DOES IT FEEL WHEN YOUR ADVANCES TOWARDS A WOMAN ARE REJECTED?

It depends on your expectations and your feelings for the woman. A rejection at a club or a disco is not the same as one where you have known the woman for years and have built up a friendship that you thought might develop further.

Graham, 19

It depends on the woman. If you're serious about her, it's like having the bottom ripped out of your world. You work up all this courage to ask her out and she slaps you in the face with it. It's the worst kind of hurt because you can't hurt back.

Gary, 22

It's a scary feeling because you can't do anything with it. If they reject you, you can't get back at them. You just have to go away feeling inadequate.

Michael, 25

Bad. I've got an ego the size of Scotland and rejection by the fairer sex cuts it down a lot. I loathe rejection — it causes you to pose painful questions about yourself.

Simon, 23

The last time it happened I wanted to run away. I couldn't be anywhere near her and I couldn't face any of my friends. I just wanted to be somewhere else.

Victor, 19

It turns your guts over.

Sean, 20

Angry — at first with her, then with myself for being such a prat.

Ian, 24

Nothing ventured nothing gained.

Jonathan, 21

You have to be rejected a few times before you can come up trumps. If you're not prepared to take a few risks you might as well curl up and become a monk.

Angus, 19

It's unbelievably hurtful. And it's almost worse when it's within the context of your relationship. Rejection from someone you're not involved with is relatively easy to brush off, but rejection from a loved one is the worst. It could be the complete, 'I'm leaving you and I love someone else' or even as simple as not wanting to have sex when you do. Both are crushing.

Allan, 30

A few men were philosophical about the need to run the risk of rejection in order to get relationships going, and were prepared to take a few knocks. Most not only expressed fear of rejection, but also anger at being rejected and frustration at not being able to cope with the feelings afterwards.

In many ways, it seems that it's men's inabilities to process these sorts of feeling that cause them either to be crippled into taking no risks at all or else acting inappropriately and expressing their frustration through anger and bitterness.

Rejection can come in a number of forms. It can be a simple refusal by a woman who's been offered a drink in a club, or it can be the final end of a love affair that's continued for a long period of time.

HAVE YOU EVER BEEN DUMPED BY A WOMAN?

No, I always make sure I do it first.

Darren, 17

Yes, who hasn't.

Richard, 20

Yes, and it's bad. You always ask why and you always get a stupid answer that you don't understand.

Lewis, 18

Yes. It's upsetting for about a week but then you just get on with it and think about where you went wrong and hope it doesn't happen next time.

Philip, 20

Yes. Excruciating.

Jason, 25

Yes. Despair and pain quickly turning to anger and then hatred.

Kapil, 20

Twice. The first time I was devastated for weeks but I wasn't particularly stable at the time. The second time I handled it better and now I think I could handle it without wallowing in self-pity.

Julian, 19

More times than I care to remember. It's easy to look back and be all sort of mature about it. But at the time you just want to scream — it's not fair!

Aaron, 22

Yes, several times. You get better at handling it each time. Either that or you learn to get in first!

Alex, 22

Yes, and if I'm honest I don't think I've ever entirely got over it. I still think of her and our relationship ended four years ago. She's married and probably very happy, but I feel a great sadness and also a lot of caution when dealing with new girlfriends. I could never love anyone like I loved her. I was obsessed. I wouldn't allow myself to fall in love like that now. I was too hurt. It made me behave stupidly for a few months afterwards. It ruined my life for a time.

James, 25

As a rule men seemed to be a lot 'cooler' on the subject of relationships than women. But that doesn't mean that they don't fall in love or become obsessed. They do. And when they do, it can be a totally consuming experience.

Some of the men mentioned their obsessive loves with a sense of great tragedy and remorse.

Have You Ever Been So Attracted To A Woman That You Became Obsessed By Her? How Did It Feel And How Did The Situation Resolve Itself?

Yes, when I was about 12, it won't happen again.

Stephen, 18

When I was about 15, I became obsessed with a married woman who lived up the road from me. She was much older than me. I used to follow her round

*town all day when I should have been at school.
I never actually spoke to her and then suddenly she
moved away from the area. I felt very stupid about the
whole business.*

Ian, 24

*Yes, it was a new girl at school. I eventually told a
mutual (girl) friend how I felt and that I would like to
go out with her. But the next time she saw me she
ignored me which upset me at first but then the feeling
of infatuation soon died.*

Robert, 19

*Yes, I think it happens to every male at some stage.
The usual result is that the feelings are not
reciprocated — which is not surprising. It happened to
me and although it was a very upsetting experience, I
learned from it. It certainly hasn't happened since.*

Justin, 22

*I was completely obsessed by my first love at 16. It
started from an obsession, but seven months later we
were going out together. Looking back it felt great, a
bit like real love, but it wasn't right, it was too one-
sided. I was too obsessed.*

Vince, 19

*After I split up with a girlfriend I used to stand outside
her work-place and wait. But I'd always leave before
she came out. I'd call her answerphone and just listen
to her message — I'd never leave one. I'd think about
her, dream about her and try and gather information
about what she was doing — like a spy. In time the
feelings passed, but I can even now feel a tug when I
think of her.*

Allan, 30

No, I'm not that stupid.

Danny, 19

No, thankfully.

Jeremy, 24

There seems to be a definite feeling among men that showing too much emotion can be a bad thing. If you show too much emotion then your friends are going to laugh at you, and if you let it get out of control it's going to become a menace to you.

Women on the other hand, at least in men's minds, actively want to promote and encourage emotions. This can be very scary and even threatening to some males.

A lot of the men seemed to be willing to admit to having gone overboard with their feelings once, and made a fool of themselves, but in so doing learnt a lesson that they were never going to repeat. It's as if once bitten – twice shy.

Many seem to think that falling desperately in love or developing an obsession is on a par with wearing a horrible anorak for most of your teens. It's something you did because you didn't know any better, and so you look back on it with embarrassment and regret.

Chapter Six

WHAT MEN THINK ABOUT SEX

Statistically speaking, men are supposed to think about sex every eight minutes. This sounds like a lot, but if it includes every time they look at a billboard advertisement featuring some scantily-clad model or glance admiringly at some pretty girl in the street or simply have a quick day-dream, then it may be possible.

A lot of sex goes on inside men's minds, but it doesn't necessarily go any further. It's fantasy sex. Sex that never becomes real. The basis for many advertising campaigns and marketing policies seems to revolve around men's abilities to fantasise about sex.

Men are not continually toying with mental pictures of full-blown sexual intercourse. It's more a case of mentally savouring the associated images of sex, by thinking about women and their bodies.

Women often ask what goes on inside men's minds when they look at an attractive woman. If they meet a stunning girl or see a seductive photograph in a magazine, do they actually fantasise about having sex with that woman?

WHEN YOU SEE A BEAUTIFUL WOMAN DO YOU FANTASISE ABOUT HAVING SEX WITH HER?

The answers vary. The majority of those interviewed said they didn't.

No. I think it's cheapening to women to consider them as sex objects.

Aaron, 22

No, certainly not.

Julian, 19

I'm not interested in fantasies like that. They're wasteful.

Angus, 19

I'd be too scared to.

Adam, 17

Those who said 'yes' qualified it:

I wouldn't get involved in a full-length fuck-fantasy, but the idea would definitely cross my mind. Probably only for a second.

Alex, 22

Yes, but not at that moment. I'd remember what she looked like and then think of her later when I was masturbating or making love.

Kevin, 24

And those who weren't certain felt the circumstances had to be right.

I'd like to say I wouldn't, because that sounds less sexist, but in reality I probably would, to some extent.

David, 21

If she really struck a chord and I had the time, like I was waiting for a bus or sitting in the doctor's waiting room, then I probably would. Give me something to do.

Lewis, 18

I might not there and then but I would maybe do it another time. Especially if I had her picture.

Michael, 25

When he sees a stunningly attractive woman a man doesn't usually conjure up some graphic image of her stripped naked with her legs wrapped round his neck. It's more likely that he will identify a strong tug of sexual arousal, and this isn't automatically manifested physically.

He won't suddenly sprout an erection or start drooling, but instead he will recognise feelings connected with sex.

Still, there are *some* men who are completely switched off to unwanted sexual stimulation, even though they are perfectly happy heterosexuals.

Most men embark on their sexual lives through masturbation. As one of the men mentioned, images of women seen during the day may provide fuel for masturbation later.

Sex is a tricky subject for men to be honest and open about and masturbation is even more difficult. During adolescence, boys may be open about masturbation and even get involved in group and mutual masturbation sessions, especially in all-male environments like boarding schools. But it very quickly becomes an embarrassing and taboo subject. Masturbation is one of those things that everybody does but no-one likes to admit to doing.

DO YOU MASTURBATE NOW? IF SO, HOW FREQUENTLY?

I used to masturbate when I was a teenager before   I was able to have real sex. Now I have a steady girlfriend, so I never do it.

Richard, 20

I don't masturbate now because I don't have to.

Vince, 19

When you're a kid you masturbate all the time. It's like you discover a new toy and can't stop playing with it. When you get older sex takes its place.

Tom, 21

Some men felt that it was merely a step along the way to real sex, a sort of practice, warm-up track that they needed back in the days when they didn't have sexually active relationships. They referred to it in the past tense as though it was something they don't do any more.

Most look upon it as a regular necessity:

It really depends on my sex life. If I'm in a relationship then I might only masturbate once a week, on average, but if I'm not then it may rise to five or six times a week.

Simon, 23

It varies on how I'm feeling — anything up to once or twice a day.

Paul, 21

Sometimes I think I wank too much. I'll do it two or three times a day. I do it more in the summer just because of the heat and the fact that every girl looks that much more sexy. It gets you going.

Nick, 18

If it's a toss-up between sex and a wank, obviously I'd go for sex. But I feel the need to empty out at least every day.

James, 21

Very rarely, probably about once a month. I don't think it is a good thing to do. I feel very guilty about it afterwards and as if I have let someone down.

Carl, 18

No-one seemed embarrassed about admitting to discovering masturbation before sex.

DID YOU MASTURBATE BEFORE YOU FIRST HAD SEX?

Of course, it was my favourite pastime for a few years before I first had sex.

Marcus, 23

Did I masturbate before I had sex?! My knob's still got finger-grooves worn into it!

Philip, 20

Like it was about to go out of fashion!

Justin, 22

Rarely. It was always followed with great feelings of guilt. It's ironic but it's only since I've been married and discussed it with my wife that I've really enjoyed masturbation!

Frank, 24

Masturbation is usually a pretty solitary and pensive pastime. Some men use magazines or videos to arouse themselves and help them through to orgasm, whereas others tend to rely on their imagination and memory.

Using magazines for stimulation is a sort of lazy fantasy. It is a ready-made, off-the-shelf fantasy in which a naked or seductively undressed woman is striking arousing poses. The masturbator can then imagine himself caressing or penetrating this complete stranger whom he has only ever known through this photographic image.

A lot of women I've discussed fantasies with, find   the idea of masturbating to a picture of a naked man completely unappealing. Some women said they have a tendency to conjure up erotic scenes in their minds which may or may not actually include penetrative sex, as though the sex side of the fantasy is optional. It's more the creation of an erotic and sensual image that is important.

On the whole, male fantasies are more basic and less erotic, revolving around penetrative sex and often simply transcribed from the pages of a magazine.

When You Masturbate Do You Ever Fantasise About A Particular Woman? Is She Someone You Know?

I fantasise about friends, celebrities and my girlfriend — there's no particular one.

Julian, 19

I fantasise about a lot of women, some famous, some not.

Richard, 20

Ex-girlfriends mainly.

Sean, 25

When you masturbate you can be with anybody in your mind. Anybody is available — that's the joy of it!

Hamish, 21

Cindy Crawford. Always Cindy Crawford.

Frank, 24

I never think of someone I know, it's always a famous model or pop star. Someone so remote that you'll never meet them.

Ian, 24

Why restrict your fantasies to people you know? I've had 'sex' with singers, sportswomen, models, even royalty!

Michael, 25

My head is full of pictures of women. I'd say that all of them are real ones, either ex-lovers or girls I work with or ones I've met. I love to lie back and touch myself, gently flicking through my mental catalogue until I find one who turns me on. Then I settle with her for a while. I might get bored and move on to another or I might flit backwards and forwards. Some may feature for just a second or else be centre-stage for the whole performance.

Kevin, 24

At the moment I think of the girl who lives in the flat downstairs. I think of her taking a bath or shaving her legs.

Peter, 20

Many men continue to masturbate regularly even when they are in active sexual relationships. For some, it is because they have developed a habit of achieving a quick convenient burst of sexual satisfaction that becomes quite addictive. It is devoid of the personal politics or accepted etiquette of sex. It's much quicker and easier and still gives the participant a bit of a buzz.

Other men may continue to masturbate because it is only during masturbation that they feel free to explore some of the fantasies they harbour. It's like being able to have sex with another woman or women without actually being physically unfaithful.

While some men indulge their fantasies during masturbation, others may feel free to indulge some of their fantasies within their relationship.

DO YOU HAVE ANY SEXUAL FANTASIES WHICH YOU'D LIKE TO EXPLORE WITH YOUR PARTNER AND HAVE YOU BEEN ABLE TO TALK TO HER ABOUT THEM? HOW DID SHE REACT?

Yes, sex outside the bedroom, different positions and sexy underwear. She agreed.

Sean, 20

No, I only lost my virginity 3 years ago – I am currently just working my way round the different

*positions but my girlfriend likes me to tell her what
I'm doing and what I'm feeling.*

Tom, 21

*No. Something is wrong if you need to have fantasies
to spice up your love life.*

Chris, 18

*Bondage and pretend rape. I'd never dare tell her
though in case she thought I was sick.*

Alex, 22

*I wanted to make love in my car at night in a busy
street with people walking by. When I told her my
heart was pounding and I went bright red. She just
thought it was funny and said yes.*

Andy, 25

I suggested anal sex. She said no. Absolutely not.

Scott, 20

*I want to have a 69-er on my sofa bed. My girlfriend
didn't know what to say but said she'd think about it.*

Darren, 19

*I want to try a three-in-a-bed sex-sandwich. But I'm
not going to tell her. No way.*

Lee, 22

The men who were willing to admit to sexual fantasies
tended to express very straightforward desires to
experiment with types of heterosexual exploration. Many
pointed out that they were reticent to communicate these
ideas to their partners because they feared being judged as
perverse. Some were pleasantly surprised to find their
partners open and unshocked by their revelations, others
felt that the whole idea of having fantasies during or
around sex was wrong, and was evidence of an
unsatisfactory sex life.

Are men judgmental of women's sexual fantasies?

HAS A SEXUAL PARTNER EVER SUGGESTED A FANTASY WHICH SHE WANTED TO INCLUDE IN YOUR LOVE-MAKING? WHAT WAS IT AND HOW DID YOU FEEL ABOUT HER SUGGESTION?

Yes, she suggested sex in her car and in her office. I was excited.

Richard, 20

She was very keen on sex outdoors which I had very little experience of. It was amazing and we made love in the strangest places. It was definitely more exciting than having sex in the bedroom, but we once got caught which was highly embarrassing.

Tom, 21

She likes to put a blindfold on me. I don't mind.

Gary, 22

She wanted to put ice-cream on my cock. I said OK as long as it wasn't strawberry.

Nick, 18

No, she's never suggested anything. I wish she would. Sort of show an interest.

Colin, 22

When it is the other way round, most men expressed surprise that their partners should have fantasies but were more than willing to co-operate.

Sex-therapists always point out that couples, as a rule, do not talk about sex and their individual needs nearly enough, if at all. This is because there is a great deal of mutual embarrassment, and even shame, connected with the topic.

DO YOU EVER DISCUSS SEX WITH YOUR PARTNER, IN TERMS OF WHAT YOU LIKE AND DISLIKE?

Most of our respondents felt they did discuss sex:

Yes, in great detail.

Julian, 19

Yes, so our sex life will improve.

Richard, 20

Yes, we are both quite open about what we find exciting and what we dislike so that we can constantly develop our sex life. If we didn't it would soon get stale and I'm sure we'd end up splitting up.

Steve, 23

Yes, usually during sex. She'll tell me where and how she wants me and I'm happy to oblige. She's a bit less keen to do what I want, but I'm glad we talk about it.

Ian, 24

Yes, but fairly indirectly. I don't think either of us would be too keen on being told exactly what to do. It's nice for me to think that she's getting exactly what she wants because we've worked it out together.

David, 21

Yes. Communication is essential so we both feel happy with all facets of the sex.

Chris, 18

We sort of joke about doing it. We give it joke names like 'playing pokey' or 'having a pickle-tickle'.

Morgan, 19

The majority of men assumed that talking about sex with their partners would aid better sex, but not every man sees it that way or feels able to enter into those sorts of discussion, often passing the 'blame' onto the woman.

Very rarely. I wish she'd be more open about it as I'd be willing to help.

Stephen, 18

No. It's not something we discuss much. She seems to be very happy with what I do at the moment.

Hamish, 21

She thinks it's dirty if I ever mention sex.

Victor, 17

No, we just get on and do it.

Martin, 22

I don't know how we'd talk about it. We do have sex but it's totally silent from start to finish and we never speak about it afterwards or say we're going to do it before. I think she's kind of shy about it. I guess I am too. I am a bit worried about if she likes it or not. I do.

Keith, 18

I've tried talking about it but she went bright red on both occasions. I think we should talk about it. She doesn't.

Neil, 22

No way. She'd think I was a perv.

Darren, 19

It seems to be far easier for men to talk about sex to women than to their male friends.

DO YOU EVER TALK INTIMATELY ABOUT SEX WITH YOUR FRIENDS?

You must be joking. I once asked a mate if he knew what I could do with a penile wart I had and he used to bring it up as a gag to tell down the pub.

James, 21

I might say whether or not I'm doing it with a particular girl. But I wouldn't go into detail. What can you say? I'd feel I was betraying her if I told secrets and I wouldn't feel too good if my friends started asking loads of intimate questions.

Mark, 19

Definitely not. It'd be a waste of time. And too much like bragging.

Neil, 22

When we were teenagers we told everything; how far she'd let us go, what colour her nipples were, how big her vagina was — everything!! But not any more. Anyone who mouths off about his girlfriend's body now is just talking generally, not specifically.

Philip, 20

I like to think I could tell my best friend everything, but sex and what actually happens when I'm doing it is like pretty sacred stuff. If I told him, I probably woudn't tell the truth.

Angus, 19

From a male point of view, the whole concept of sex is often confused by people not telling the truth. Too much of what men grow up learning about sex comes from unreliable sources, namely other men.

One typically myth-ridden subject is the orgasm.

For men, both sex and masturbation culminate in an orgasm. The 'come' is the big finale of most men's sexual activities, mainly because they find it very difficult to continue the same sort of activity after coming as their erection subsides and the penis becomes limp. Men normally achieve orgasm much more easily and mechanically than women.

In many ways it's less of a big deal to men than it is to women. Many men will reach orgasm within their first few adolescent attempts at masturbation, and from then on there's no looking back. Yet many women never experience an orgasm until they are into their 20s although they may have already had penetrative sexual intercourse.

If a young man is masturbating two or three times a day, the chances are he will be achieving orgasm every time. So, if it's such a mechanical and readily available sensation, do men value it? What does it feel like?

HOW WOULD YOU DESCRIBE THE FEELING OF HAVING AN ORGASM?

It's like having the life-blood drained out of you. When I come I feel like I've been turned inside out.

Gary, 22

Sometimes it makes me feel sad. Sort of depressed.

Antonio, 23

It's a rush. A force ten gale blowing out your balls.

Danny, 19

Orgasms are too short and too intense. They'd be better if they lasted longer and were more manageable.

Sam, 20

The trouble with coming is that you spend so much of the time telling yourself not to come so you can keep on humping. So when you do come you feel like you've done something wrong.

Darryl, 22

It's hot and wet.

Ryan, 18

If it's done right it's like scoring a winning goal: you're running up the pitch, weaving and dodging, getting closer to the penalty area, and the crowd start getting louder and louder reaching a crescendo and then roar, just as you triumphantly punt the ball majestically into the back of the net.

Jeremy, 24

It doesn't feel like that much. The build-up's best.

Stephen, 18

Obviously some men feel that some orgasms can be pretty spectacular events, but generally they don't hold the same mystique as the female orgasm because they are so easily achieved. There is also the added complication of premature ejaculation, where men feel guilty for reaching orgasm during sex too quickly.

The sex orgasm comes loaded with expectation and pressure inasmuch as it's supposed to be choreographed in order to fit in with the female's needs. On the other hand, the masturbation come is a quick, self-satisfying snack.

IS THE EXPERIENCE OF HAVING AN ORGASM FROM MASTURBATION THE SAME AS AN ORGASM DURING SEX?

It's the same, only sex is better.

Lewis, 18

I wish it was the same. I can last for hours when I'm masturbating, but when I'm having sex I just want to come straight off.

Morgan, 19

There's no difference in your body, only what's in your head.

Maurice, 18

A sex come is much more intense and much more exciting. It could make you shout out. A wank come is just like flossing your teeth.

Max, 21

Many women state that they often do not achieve orgasm during penetrative sex. Men usually do:

WHEN YOU MAKE LOVE DO YOU ALWAYS ACHIEVE ORGASM?

Always. I can't see the point of all that work if you don't come at the end of it.

Peter, 20

Being a man, ejaculation is the whole point of sex. I've never had sex without orgasm.

Chris, 24

Almost always. Not coming leaves me unsatisfied and uptight which is not the idea of sex to my mind.

Darryl, 22

Usually yes. Except I remember on one occasion when I'd had some E and I kept at it for ages and my girlfriend was really enjoying it but no matter what I did I couldn't come. In the end I gave up on it.

Stephen, 18

No, not always. Sometimes I'm too involved in making sure my wife has an orgasm and miss out on my own.

James, 21

Those who didn't always achieve orgasm felt it was an exception rather than a general rule.

As for women's orgasms, most men seemed very concerned although not necessarily that knowledgeable.

When You Make Love Does Your Partner Always Achieve Orgasm?

I don't really know. I hope so, and she does sound like she's enjoying it. But I'm not 100% sure that she always comes. And I know you're not supposed to ask.

Lee, 22

Yes, I always make sure that she does.

Simon, 23

Usually, but sometimes she lets me know that she's not going to come and that that's all right.

Gerry, 26

No, my current girlfriend was a virgin when we met and she has not yet had an orgasm. I don't think.

Raj, 21

Yes, we usually both achieve orgasm at the same time because we've worked out exactly what works for both of us.

Aaron, 22

I don't know.

Morgan, 19

The female's feelings about reaching orgasm were similarly unexplored for many men:

How Important Is It To Her That She Has An Orgasm?

We've never really discussed it.

Tim, 20

I don't know, she refuses to discuss it with me.

Jonathan, 21

*I'm not sure if she does and she certainly won't say —
at least she hasn't.*

Andy, 25

*She would like to have one and sometimes feels
frustrated that she can't.*

Gerry, 26

*Vital. She always expects me to continue until she has
achieved at least one orgasm. Even if I've come I will
stimulate her until she does.*

Philip, 20

Very important — but then it's important to me too.
Sean, 20

HOW IMPORTANT IS IT TO YOU THAT YOUR PARTNER HAS AN ORGASM?

Very. Otherwise I would feel I'd let her down.

Sean, 20

*I see it as a goal that shows me I have succeeded in
satisfying her. I derive more pleasure from making her
happy than from my own orgasm.*

Julian, 19

*Vitally important. I would feel that I had not made
love properly if I left her unsatisfied and it would spoil
it for me.*

Mel, 23

*I feel a very poor lover if I can't give a woman at least
one orgasm for every one of mine. It's an insult to my
technique if they don't come and completely spoils it
for me.*

John, 24

It's not my problem.

Nick, 18

Men want their partners to experience orgasms because they want to be able to feel that they've performed their sexual function successfully and adeptly.

Men view the female orgasm with awe and mystique as though it were something rare and elusive that only good lovers and real men are able to 'give' to a woman.

There is a danger that women's orgasms will become another unfathomable aspect of the whole myth of sex that grows in some men's minds. Men think that successful orgasms equal women's pleasure and the degree of women's pleasure equals the sexual expertise of that man. There is a scene in the film WHEN HARRY MET SALLY in which the actress simulates an orgasm verbally in a restaurant. This was a worry to many men as they don't like to think women are faking. For many, if you can't make a woman come then you can't be a real man.

Sadly, fears about inadequacy and potential ridicule can lead to sexual problems. Young men have to carry quite a burden of expectation with them when they enter into sexual relations with women. They feel they're supposed to be well-hung and well-versed in the sophisticated intricacies of sexual intercourse.

In some interviews I conducted on radio recently, I asked groups of teenage boys about their views on male virginity. It was almost as though I was talking about something which didn't exist. Practically no-one would admit to being a virgin – the stigma was too great.

You are pressurised into pretending that you're not a virgin from an early age. This makes it impossible to ask your peers for advice because the chances are they don't know anything anyway because they're lying about their own experiences, and by asking you'll only end up making yourself into a laughing stock because you've been foolish enough to come clean about your inexperience.

Pressure is a problem. Some men feel under pressure to be a good lover even though they might never have had sex before.

DO YOU EVER FEEL APPREHENSIVE BEFORE SEX THAT YOU MIGHT NOT BE ABLE TO SATISFY YOUR PARTNER?

Every time I first have sex with a woman I get very nervous that I won't be able to get an erection or that I might come too quickly but after a few times I feel more relaxed.

Alex, 22

Yes, who doesn't.

Graham, 19

Sometimes I feel I've got to do a good job, especially if the woman is particularly beautiful or means a lot to me, but it soon evaporates once I get started.

Tom, 21

Never. I've not had any complaints so far.

Chris, 18

No, exactly the opposite.

Keith, 18

No, because we discuss sex in detail and we both know what satisfies each other.

Tim, 20

Sometimes I've experienced my penis going limp just before entry. I always think it's because I'm thinking too much about what I'm doing rather than just relaxing and enjoying it. I have learnt that if this happens, it'll be all right again in a short while. But it's difficult if it's the first time with this girl. It's not something you feel like having to explain.

Darryl, 22

I get it into my head that she's had loads of boyfriends and they all know how to do things I don't. This can really cramp your style.

Vince, 19

> *My guts start churning and I hate it. The thing I hate most is that I'm supposed to know what to do and when. There's never any talk and the girl just lies there waiting for me to make all the moves. But no-one ever tells you when you're supposed to do what.*

Paul, 21

The most common sexual problems that men suffer from are premature ejaculation and impotence.

HAVE YOU EVER HAD ANY SEXUAL PROBLEMS SUCH AS IMPOTENCE OR PREMATURE EJACULATION? HOW DID YOUR PARTNER REACT? IS THIS STILL A PROBLEM?

> *Coming too soon. She was disappointed. No.*

Carl, 18

> *No. No complaints.*

Kieran, 26

> *None. Everything's been pretty much like clockwork.*

Scott, 20

> *Sometimes I'd lose my erection if I got real het-up. Now I've learnt to keep cool.*

David, 21

> *Only once. One night I couldn't get an erection which worried me at the time but my girlfriend was very good about it and it's never happened again.*

Simon, 23

> *When I was much younger I always used to come before I wanted to which would sometimes annoy my girlfriend at the time but more recently it's not been a problem — probably because I feel less anxious about sex than I used to.*

Sean, 25

Most respondents denied that there was ever any problem in their sex life. And a lot answered along the same lines as the masturbation issue — 'It's something that used to happen but I've grown out of that now.'

Apart from the obvious embarrassment and 'loss of cred' that a sexual problem might engender, it is difficult for men to know how and where to deal with the issue.

IF YOU EVER HAD A SEXUAL PROBLEM WHICH YOU DID NOT THINK YOU COULD SOLVE ON YOUR OWN, WHERE WOULD YOU FIRST GO FOR HELP?

My girlfriend.

James, 21

My GP.

Robert, 19

I'd consult some books on sex and then a doctor if I couldn't sort it out.

Kapil, 20

I'd probably phone one of those sex-help phonelines from the back of Knave or Fiesta or something.

Morgan, 19

I wouldn't go anywhere. I'd be too embarrassed. I'd learn to deal with it myself — somehow.

Darren, 19

I might ask my sister or maybe my closest friend. I wouldn't be worried that he'd split on me. I just wouldn't be too sure that he'd know any better than me.

Jeremy, 24

A doctor. A private one probably.

Jeff, 28

Some men do resort to writing to a few of the problem pages and agony columns that now deal with male letters. Most of the letters that I receive about specific sexual problems tend to be requests for advice on how to deal with premature ejaculation and pleas for information on increasing penis size.

On the subject of sexuality, rather than just sex, one of the most frequent 'problem letters' I get from young men is about a fear of being gay. The most common letter usually relates some sort of physical encounter or sexual fantasy that has occurred involving another male which has led them to fear that they might be gay. Aspects of homosexuality or effeminacy are so often used as terms of abuse amongst males of all ages that a phobia has developed, certainly among adolescents.

WHAT ARE YOUR VIEWS ON HOMOSEXUALITY?

Everyone should be free to express their sexuality though it's not my particular preference.

Julian, 19

I think that it is terrible that there is a different age of consent for gays. This merely makes homosexuality different and therefore deviant. If the ages matched there might be less resistance.

Maurice, 18

I think it's unnatural but as long as they don't force it onto anybody else then it's their business.

Simon, 23

I do not like the idea of it.

Tim, 20

As a Christian I am completely opposed to it but I think those who suffer from it should be treated with compassion and sympathy.

Martin, 22

It totally disgusts me. I think queers should be treated with drugs to try and cure them.

Carl, 18

The most common response was along the lines of 'they're fine so long as they keep themselves to themselves'.

According to statistics most males will have had some form of homosexual experience during their formative years; anything ranging from experimental touching or looking to mutual masturbation or even sex. This does not necessarily mean that they go on to be practising homosexuals, it is merely a very common part of normal male development.

HAVE YOU EVER HAD ANY SEXUAL EXPERIENCES WITH OTHER MEN?

No.

Lewis, 18

Never.

Alex, 22

I once French kissed a mate at a party for a bet. That's all that happened.

Stephen, 18

When I was young I shared a bed with a cousin on holiday in Cornwall and we did some mutual fondling and masturbation. I felt very guilty about it.

Steven, 23

I've touched another boy's cock. But I'm not gay.

Adam, 19

I've been in bed with another bloke and a girl. We both had sex with her but we never did anything to each other.

Bryan, 27

A small minority of respondents admitted that they had had a homosexual experience, but none voiced it as a prospect for the future.

IS IT SOMETHING YOU MIGHT CONSIDER IN FUTURE?

The thought repulses me.

Chris, 18

There is no way I would ever have sex with a man.   I would rather die first.

Vince, 19

Definitely not.

Richard, 20

It's not on my list of top ten ambitions — but then, never say never.

Hamish, 21

I certainly don't plan to.

Adam, 19

Totally no way.

Stephen, 18

Through advertising and the media, men are bombarded with images of sex. They are fed on a diet   of sexual fantasy and make-believe which, not surprisingly, rather warps their perception of it all.

If you add this to the fact that most of them have been subject to a lot of peer pressure and misinformation from an early age, it's not surprising that many of them are either very confused or very shy or very misguided about sex.

Overall the impression is that men are generally just a bit frightened of sex and women and of women's expectations of them. They're frightened that their experience of sex and women will make them look and feel even more inadequate than they (often secretly) feel already.

Chapter Seven

WHAT MEN THINK OF WORK

To a lot of men, their career is a very important part of their identity. 'What d'you do for a living?' is a sort of standard conversational question. And it is asked because the answer is supposed to give some sort of measure of the man. It's supposed to tell the person asking certain things about his character and personality. In theory it gives a reflection of his ambitions, his intellect, his attitude and his social standing.

In some circles the same is also true of women; career and work have become symbols of character, career achievements have become badges of 'success'.

Given that there is this notion of 'you are what you do', how concerned are men about what they do?

HOW IMPORTANT IS YOUR WORK TO YOU?

The majority rated it highly:

Very. I never thought I'd ever hear myself say that, but it's true. I like my job and I take a lot of pride in being good at it.

Marcus, 23

A lot of people rely on me to get it right. If I don't we're all sunk. So I take it seriously. You've got to.

Justin, 22

Immensely important. Work is my passport to a better life. If I work hard and do well I can start to have the things I really want.

Neil, 22

*My career is important because I can see some
direction in it and I can see development and progress
as I get promoted. Yes, it gives me the feelings of
achievement and power.*

Chris, 24

*It takes up a large part of our lives — certainly mine.
So it has to be satisfying and it has to be important.*

Sean, 25

It's important because if I didn't have it I'd go mad.

Sam, 24

More important than anything else at the moment.

Michael, 25

A significant minority saw it as a necessary evil:

*It's a good laugh, I like the gang I'm with, but if I won
the Pools, that's it. I'm chucking it in — straight off.*

Vince, 19

Work gets me money. Money buys you freedom.

Gerry, 26

*I like being out of the house and being surrounded
by good lads but the work itself is bollocks.*

David, 21

*It's not important to anybody. It is important to do it
though, because without work you only get dole.*

Jonathan, 21

A few hated it:

My work makes me sick. It's not important, it's shit.

Kapil, 20

*It's not so important, I'd do anything rather than go to
work.*

Keith, 17

The fruits of male toil are most frequently gauged in terms of money and power. Power can take the form of freedom or authority or it can be linked directly to money and take the form of spending-power. Some men measure their success purely in terms of money and power.

But what about power in work itself? Do men automatically desire more power?

WOULD YOU LIKE A JOB WHERE YOU COULD EXERCISE MORE POWER?

Most said yes:

Yes of course. Power equals money and status.

Jonathan, 21

Yes, I would like to have more influence over the decisions made at work but that doesn't mean I want power for power's sake. Anyone who feels like that usually wants to abuse the power they have.

Simon, 23

Yes. I get so pissed off at work when I'm continually being told what to do by idiots who know less about my job than I do. I don't really want power over other people, just over my own area of work.

Martin, 22

Most of the time I feel like a dogsbody. It's degrading. I'm not saying that I'm better than anyone, but if I had more power I'd use it more effectively and more kindly than some of the tossers who have it.

Paul, 21

Yes. Because there's a few people I'd give the sack to right off if I could.

Victor, 17

No, I would like to be consulted more, where people took my advice, but I wouldn't want to exploit them or have power over them. That's just sick.

Bryan, 28

No, not at all. I don't like to be powerful at work and the less power I have over other people the better.

Julian, 19

IN YOUR WORKING LIFE, HOW IMPORTANT IS MONEY?

I need money to live, that's how I see it. As long as I can survive on my money then I'm happy.

Darryl, 22

Not at all important. If you do something well and enjoy it then money doesn't really matter and you'll usually find that money follows anyway.

Hamish, 21

In the long term money is the reason for choosing a career. The amount of money you have access to determines the way you can live. I want to live in the best possible fashion.

James, 21

Important — you need money to provide for others.

Stephen, 18

Vital. What's the point of working if you don't get paid well? If you have to work then you might as well do the job that pays the most.

Carl, 18

Very important. It seems very difficult in this world to do things without money. If you've got something to fall back on you can enjoy life more.

Andy, 25

If you've got money you've got choices. Without it you're weak.

Jeremy, 24

And if money is a symbol of power, does it follow that a man is going to feel emasculated or stripped of his power if the woman in his life has got access to more money?

HOW WOULD YOU FEEL IF YOUR WIFE OR GIRLFRIEND EARNED MORE MONEY THAN YOU?

Embarrassed and second-rate.

Jonathan, 21

Unacceptable. I just couldn't handle it, the relationship would have to end.

Raj, 21

It's very unlikely but I wouldn't be very happy if it did happen.

Graham, 19

If she earned more than me I'd expect her to pull her weight more. I wouldn't want her to end up being the boss, though.

John, 24

I'd be pleased for her but I wouldn't like it much. Out of the two of us I feel I should be the bread-winner — which is wrong — but I suppose it's my male ego coming out there.

Michael, 25

I'd think 'good for her' and help her spend it.

Paul, 18

She already does. I'm proud of her. She's a very clever lady. I've no problem telling friends she's the one who brings home the bacon. Doesn't mean I wouldn't want to do it myself, though.

Liam, 29

I don't think it matters at all. My mum's always earned more money than my dad. He's had lots of times out of work but she's had a steady job. It's quite normal and it doesn't mean he's any worse because of it. If it happened to me I wouldn't think anything of it.

Adam, 17

She does already and it doesn't bother me.

Tom, 21

I wouldn't even think about it. Money is immaterial, or should be, in a relationship.

Kieran, 26

There seems to be a reasonable agreement among men that the convention of the male being the principal provider is changing. As women's position in society and the workplace strengthens, so men have to change their perceptions of both women's power and themselves.

But how far are they prepared to go?

DO YOU THINK IT IS RIGHT FOR MEN TO STAY AT HOME AND LOOK AFTER THE KIDS WHILE MEN GO OUT TO WORK?

If they're both content with the situation then fair enough. But I would never let it happen.

Raj, 21

If some men are happy doing that then fine, but not me. No way.

James, 25

Sure it's right enough, but I wouldn't wish any children to be stuck in my care for the day. They'd never survive.

Liam, 29

I think lots of blokes start off doing it, but they can't stick it. They need to get out and do physical work.

Ryan, 18

I think in the family set-up it's not essential for either partner to take the role of bread-winner. If one has to work then the other can look after the kids whether male or female.

Mark, 19

Yes, and why not? I'd be perfectly happy to do that.

Darrell, 21

Yes, I don't see any problems with that. In fact I'd quite like to do that at some stage in my life.

Julian, 19

Sometimes I get on my knees and pray that I could be a house-husband. The idea of spending the day watching Neighbours *and* Pebble Mill *while munching microwave popcorn fills me with glee. But I guess in reality it's not like that, and anyway, we all get bored with everything eventually.*

James, 21

The concept of man as house-husband seemed to receive mixed reactions. Many respondents saw the positive possibilities of a lifestyle that didn't involve having to go out to work every day. The main argument against it was that men wouldn't be able to do it well enough, as opposed to men shouldn't do it.

It is becoming more common for women to be in charge at work, which does put some men in a subordinate position.

HOW WOULD YOU FEEL HAVING A WOMAN FOR A BOSS?

Most were in favour:

I've worked for men and women as bosses and I definitely preferred the latter. She was more fair.

Justin, 22

I'd have no problem with that at all.

Julian, 19

Fine, there is no reason why a woman couldn't do the job, probably do it better than a man.

Andy, 25

A few were very against it:

It wouldn't be feasible. Where I work there is a strict male hierarchical system. A woman entering it would throw everything out of tilt.

Frank, 24

I've never met a woman who could do my boss's job. I don't believe there is one.

Antonio, 23

Demoralised and dejected. If I wanted to work for a woman I could have got a job in a chemist shop.

Gerry, 26

Because work is an important source of identity and worth for a lot of men, it is also a breeding ground for competition and jealousy. It's one thing to want your fellow man to see that you're doing well in your chosen field, but it's a totally different thing being able to accept *his* success gracefully without feeling pangs of envy.

HOW IMPORTANT IS IT THAT YOU'RE DOING BETTER AT YOUR CAREER THAN YOUR FRIENDS ARE AT THEIRS?

I know it sounds mean, but when I hear that someone's got promoted or got a raise in salary, I feel kind of funny. I want to be happy for them, especially if it's someone I like, but I also feel strange and a bit bad if they're doing better than me.

Michael, 25

If they're in a different business — fine, I don't give a toss. If they're in my line of sales, they're the enemy.

Amin, 23

All my friends are doing much better than me in money terms, but I finish early, so maybe it balances out.

Tom, 21

I don't discuss business with friends. I don't announce how I'm doing and I don't really want to know about them. It's much safer that way.

Sean, 25

A bit of competition's healthy but no-one takes it too seriously.

Peter, 20

Nothing seems to arouse the competitive spirit so much as work. So, when one man asks another man conversationally what he does for a living, it doesn't necessarily open up a whole new web of communication and conversational topics. Instead it often raises a lot of issues of competition, secrecy and jealousy. Instead of bringing two men closer together, it can quite easily force them apart.

Chapter Eight

THE NEW MAN

During the late '80s, the concept of the 'New Man' was created by newspapers and magazines. The New Man was portrayed as a modern breed of male who has developed a deep sensitivity and emotional awareness that was sadly missing in the old man. The New Man was an all-thinking, all-feeling guy who wasn't sexist, racist or prejudiced. But a few years down the line does this new man as outlined above actually exist?

If there is such a thing as a New Man, what do men think he is like?

How Would You Describe The 'New Man'?

The 'New Man' is supposed to be non-sexist, supportive, understanding, trustworthy, caring to all those around him and a generally fun guy too.

Mark, 19

I wish the term had never been invented. It conjures up images of men in polo-neck jumpers changing nappies and talking about their feelings. Which apart from sounding naff is probably about as appealing to a woman as having sex with a kipper.

Kevin, 24

He is merely the description of a man who has always existed to a greater or lesser extent. Someone who believes in equality and a meritocracy, who holds no ill-judged and preconceived ideas about women.

Julian, 19

I think a New Man is a bloke who is non-sexist, non-racist, shares his feelings, expresses his anger and doesn't try to took down girls' blouses.

Nick, 18

As a myth. He doesn't exist in reality, he was cooked up by the media.

Marcus, 23

Queer?

Lee, 22

A wanker — I don't know anyone in their right mind who would want to be one.

Frank, 24

The majority of men interviewed felt that the New Man was a bit of a middle-class poncy know-it-all, or else he was gay.

Some felt that even the concept of there being such a thing as a New Man was an attack on them. It was tantamount to saying they were the old 'wrong' model and that there was a 'better' new model being developed. So, they reacted by being defensive or attacking in return. And as is quite common with males of all ages, one well-tried means of attack is to comment on a man's sexuality, specifically to accuse him of being homosexual.

Only a very small percentage thought that he was just an ordinary man who has been there all along but doesn't feel a need to be macho in the conventional manner.

In the same way, the notion of Feminism seemed to have been translated into something potentially negative.

WHAT IS A FEMINIST?

A lesbian.

Morgan, 19

A woman who wants men to have less power and women to have top jobs and higher wages.

Colin, 22

*Some woman with short spikey hair, big boots and a
bad attitude about men.*

Darren, 18

*A Feminist is a person, a man or a woman, who
basically believes women are better than men and
that they should get a better deal.*

Bryan, 28

A mouthy dyke.

James, 25

An angry woman.

Hamish, 21

*A man or woman who believes in equal rights for
women.*

Aaron, 22

*Feminists are women who want to rule the country —
like Mrs Thatcher.*

Nick, 18

*True Feminists are people devoted to the cause of
achieving equal rights for women at any costs. But the
modern interpretation of a Feminist is just anyone
who's against sexism or the treating of women purely
as sex objects.*

Kevin, 24

Most of the respondents believed that all Feminists were
women. And interestingly, as with the attacks on New Men
being gay or effeminate, the attack on Feminists was that
they had to be gay or *unfeminine*.

Even the men who felt that Feminists could be either
male or female, were still largely of the understanding that
Feminists wanted to prove women were 'better' than men,
or that they wanted to 'rule' men. The notion of equality
was only mentioned by a very few.

When they were asked about their attitudes to doing chores and duties that were traditionally the domain of women, surprisingly few were anti.

DO YOU DO HOUSEHOLD CHORES LIKE WASHING, CLEANING AND COOKING? OR DO YOU THINK OF THESE AS WOMEN'S WORK?

I don't do any cleaning but I do my own washing sometimes and I can cook easy meals. I don't think they're especially women's work because we all have to eat and wear clothes — don't we?

Philip, 20

My mum does everything. She wouldn't let me do anything even if I wanted to. I suppose it is women's work except cooking, my dad is a catering manager and used to be a chef. But he doesn't do any cooking at home.

Adam, 19

My mum works so we all have to help out at home. I do a bit of everything but not cooking. No, it's not women's work.

Tom, 21

Since I've lived on my own I've had to do all my own housework and cleaning. Of course it's not women's work.

Sean, 25

My wife does most of the work around the house. I take care of the garden and the car and the garage. I don't think cleaning and cooking was designed specifically for women to do, but I think even my wife would agree that in her case anyway, she's better suited.

Michael, 25

I have flatmates, we have a rota of chores and everyone does everything. Cleaning may have been delegated as women's work but that was when they didn't go out to work.

Simon, 23

I cook, very well, and I do some cleaning, but I take my washing home to my mother. She has a machine and I can't iron.

Paul, 21

I am self-sufficient. I wouldn't want or expect a woman to do my chores.

Mel, 23

My sisters and my mum do the cleaning. My dad looks after the car and I help out in the garden. If you asked them they'd say they're happier doing the indoor stuff.

Pat, 19

I live on my own. Who else would do it? It's stupid and sexist to say cleaning and cooking is women's work.

Richard, 20

My mum can't cook to save her life. But she has got a good job, she's a Personnel Manager. That's her work, not cleaning.

Jeff, 26

Necessity is the mother of invention, and modern circumstances dictate that in many households women are not available to do all the 'traditional' household duties, because they are out at work themselves.

Many young men are growing up with this situation and so they are learning from an early age to contribute to the household chores. Those who are contributing don't seem to voice any resentment. No-one actually said that they thought cleaning was women's work per se, a couple thought women were 'better suited' to it or did it out of preference to other sorts of chores.

The term New Man seems to have put a certain amount of fear into men or else just got their backs up. But the role of the man in both a domestic and social context is changing, partly through necessity and partly through cultural development. Therefore many of the men who claimed to dislike the New Man could be described as one.

The concept of New Man, whether he exists or not, has caused a degree of confusion amongst some men. They are now unsure how they are expected to behave with women and with each other.